Feeling Good & Living Great

How Handling Any Feeling Well
Helps You Live a Better Life

Dr. Lisa Love

Ageless Publications
Ojai, CA.

Copyright © 2011 by Ageless Publications
and Dr. Lisa Love

All rights reserved.
This book is sold subject to the condition that it shall not, by way of trade or otherwise, be lent, re-sold, hired out, or otherwise circulated without the publisher's prior consent in any form of binding or cover other than that in which it was purchased. Also, no part of this publication may be reproduced or transmitted in any form, or by any means, electronic or mechanical, including photocopy, recording, computer, or any information storage and retrieval system, without permission in writing from the publisher.

Cover & Inside Art Work:
Public domain from Microsoft Publisher.

Requests for permission to make copies of any part of this work should be mailed to:

Dr. Lisa Love
lisa@doctorlisalove.com

Get help with the teachings in this book directly from Dr. Lisa Love.

To learn more about Coaching, Books, Seminars, Teleclasses visit:

Website:
www.doctorlisalove.com

Social Media:
www.facebook.com/drlisalove
www.twitter.com/doctorlisalove
www.youtube.com/doctorlisalove

**This book is joyfully dedicated to
all those who seek to live with greater
love, clarity, compassion, energy,
fulfillment, and joy!**

Table of Contents

Part One: No Bad Feelings	7
Feelings 101	17
The Role of the Witness	33
Thinking it Over	43
Handling Feelings Well	59
Part Two: The Major Feeling States	75
Shifting Fear into Love	79
Shifting Confusion into Clarity	97
Shifting Sorrow into Compassion	113
Shifting Anger into Energy	127
Shifting Jealousy into Fulfillment	143
Shifting Happiness into Joy	157
Part Three: Emotional Rescue Tools	171
Putting it All Together	193

Part One

No Bad Feelings

Feeling Good & Living Great

Have you ever wondered why some people seem to do well in life, even if they have gone through a series of difficult times? Yet, others, who may not have experienced nearly as many hardships, are easily dragged down? How can this be? And, how can you be one of the people who moves through life feeling good and living great no matter what events may occur?

In many ways it's simple! In fact it is a secret that many joyful people know well. For them there are no bad feelings. They welcome anger, jealousy, confusion, sorrow, and even fear. Why? Because they have discovered how to get the gift out of every feeling. And, in viewing feelings as a signal to get moving to find the gold, they are able to transform their feelings so that they can live no matter what with more love, clarity, compassion, energy, fulfillment, and joy.

That gold, that gift, can never be found, however, if you are busy saying there are good and bad feelings, or emotions. The secret isn't to move from something like anger to a state of happiness. The secret is to discover what anger is trying to teach you. And, by the way, even happiness can be a good or bad emotion. Think about it. Plenty of people feel happy at the same time they are doing destructive things like indulging in addictive and manic behaviors that cause them not to live great in the long run.

So why do so many people believe there are good and bad feelings? Usually because most people don't know how to work with their feeling states well. They don't know how to catch that feeling state when it is relatively harmless. Instead, they wait until the feeling becomes an emotion. An "e-motion" is energy in motion. And, how you direct that energy determines whether events in life lift you up or bring you down. They decide whether you live in a positive way or in a living hell.

In fact, it has already been stated by some that your capacity to manage your feelings or emotions well, is a greater determiner of success than intelligence. Why? Because feelings provide the link between intellect and action. When they are linked up well to both (and even further to your spiritual essence), your feelings provide a clear channel for intelligent and wise action in the world.

They also motivate you, or move you, which is why they are referred to as the power factor of your being. They give you the power to move in a certain direction. When you lack that motivation, or don't have the ability to handle the events of life well on an emotional level, it doesn't matter how brilliant you are. Your ideas and intentions will fail to manifest because on an emotional level you will blow your opportunities up. And, it doesn't even matter if you do become successful in your career, with money, or in other areas of your life. Why? Because if you fail to manage your anger, sorrow, confusion, fear, jealousy, and happiness well (because your happiness comes at the expense of others), then you will fail to feel good and likewise fail to live a truly great life.

It doesn't have to be like this. You can learn to handle any feeling in a positive way. You can access various feeling states and use them effectively to get motivated and stay motivated, giving you the energy you need to make breakthroughs and live a life that really makes you feel good because you are living great from a state of energy, compassion, love, clarity, fulfillment, and joy.

But first, let me give you a basic understanding of why feelings are such an important factor in your life. Maybe you have heard of the law of attraction, the notion that what you think and believe tends to manifest in your life. You might have also learned techniques like visualizations, affirmations, creating vision boards, and setting intentions all designed to help you get what you want.

So far, so good, especially if (as my book *Beyond the Secret: Spiritual Power and the Law of Attraction* indicates) you learn to align your intentions and wishes in life with what is in your highest and best interests in the long run. But, as many people who practice the law of attraction know, despite all your efforts you may discover that things still don't manifest. You still don't attract what you intend to. You still remain sluggish and unmotivated. And, no matter how hard you affirm it to be otherwise, nothing ever changes in your life. More puzzling, at times your life may even get worse.

Well, consider this! It's a childhood game called *Kerplunk* that illustrates why a failure to handle your feelings well may stop you from attracting what you want so you can move forward in the direction you intend to. The use of the *Kerplunk* game as a metaphor for how feelings work in conjunction with the law of attraction was first illustrated in Michael Losier's book *The Law of Attraction*. The game consists of a tube, marbles, pickup sticks and a tray. The object of the game is to get the marbles to the bottom of the tube. Or, in this case to get the intentions (marbles) to manifest as results (tray). Consider the below:

>*Tube = Alignment With Spirit*
>*Marbles = Thoughts & Intentions*
>*Pickup Sticks = Feelings & Emotions*
>*Tray = Actions Following Through*

Notice to play the game in the most effective way you need to add in a few other factors besides the marbles and tray. You also need the to deal with the tube and the pickup sticks. So let's play the game a new way. To begin with make sure what you want is aligned with what Spirit wants for you. In other words, take time to find out if what you are trying to attract is in your highest and best interests in the long run. (To learn more about these steps check out my book *Beyond the Secret: Spiritual Power and the Law of Attraction*). Making sure you are playing for what is best in the long run, not just the short run, helps you stay in alignment (the tube stays straight), ensuring that what you attract now will help you feel good and live great not only in the present, but the future.

So far, so good. Moving a step further you still

have one more factor to contend with — the pickup sticks — or all those feelings you are not handling well that keep you stuck. For example, let's say you have the intention to lose twenty pounds, make more money, or find the love of your life. If all goes well, you do in fact lose weight, attract more money, and meet that special someone. But, too often, no matter how much you try, the weight stays put, the money stream remains low, and the love of your life is no where to be found.

How can this be? Are you failing to visualize and affirm enough about what you want? Do you need to get your intentions more clear? Maybe, but probably not. Yes, at times your limiting beliefs may prevent you from even putting the marbles (your positive intentions) into the tube. And, you may need to get your marbles together more by tweaking your affirmations, or getting more specific about what you want on your vision board. You may even need to rethink your intentions so they come from a more spiritual and less egotistical space meaning they fit in the tube in the first place.

But, more than likely these fixes alone won't help. Despite all your intentions, affirmations, and visioning, the marbles may just sit there, stuck! Why? Because your mishandling of your feelings is sabotaging your efforts. As seen in the *Kerplunk* game every time you fail to direct your emotions (the pickup sticks) in a healthy and productive way nothing moves because you fail to get motivated in the right way. Sitting there stagnant, sabotaging your ability to follow through or act appropriately, your feelings and emotions fail to serve you. No matter how hard you try, nothing works out as you hope it will.

That's why feelings or emotions are considered "*the power factor of manifestation.*" They e-mote you into the direction you need to go. When used spiritually they also move you into the direction Spirit wants you to go. And, that is why the name of the game isn't just about setting intentions and thinking positive. Nor, is it about getting rid of bad feelings and only having good ones (namely happy ones). The name of the game is knowing how to use any feeling in the right way to move you into the right direction so you can live a joy filled life.

Why do I say *any* feeling? Because even feelings like fear, confusion, sorrow, anger, and jealousy can result in some good. As this book reveals there are no good and bad feelings. As you will learn so-called bad feelings like anger if used in a healthy way can help you set necessary boundaries and give you more focus and energy. And, so-called good feelings like happiness if used in unhealthy ways can lead to negative results like self-indulgence and addictions if you are not careful.

That is why I have often stated that all feelings have a gift to give you, and all feelings are your friends. They all have something to teach you. Acting as if you must only have good feelings is erroneous. Living this way can even cause you to lose your humanity, your sensitivity, and your capacity to live life fully. People who have been encouraged to "act happy" and "cheer up" after the loss of a loved one, or after they have experienced something traumatic, know how insensitive it feels to have someone say these words. That is why it is far better to feel all your feelings and emote them in an effective and spiritually powerful way, instead of trying to get rid of them or numb them out. When you learn to work with your emotions in a healthy way you will be able to shift:

> *Fear into Love*
> *Confusion into Clarity*
> *Sorrow into Compassion*
> *Anger into Energy*
> *Jealousy into Fulfillment*
> *Happiness into Joy*

And, when you know how to emote any feeling in a healthy way you will no longer feel the pressure to live life artificially where you pretend you don't feel certain feelings. You also won't get stuck in the trap of pretending that to live a great life you should only feel happiness, with all other feelings regulated to a dark corner where they are ignored or despised.

What happens when you treat feelings this way? Let's take anger. True, anger is very destructive if handled poorly. But, if you turn your anger into energy so you can make a positive difference in the world it can become very useful. Examples include the MADD movement (Mothers Against Drunk Drivers) who turned their pain and anger over having their loved ones killed by drunk drivers into an educational campaign to stop drunk driving.

Let's move to another example, sorrow. What happens when you don't feel your sorrow and fake being happy instead? You become either clingy and neurotic, or one of the most insensitive and cruel people around. Why? Because sorrow is meant to teach you to widen your view and expand your heart. It is there to sensitize you to the suffering of others and season you with a healthy dose of compassion. Freeze off that sorrow and put a happy face on it and you get the cruel comments so popular especially in law of attraction circles such as how you must have attracted that bad experience to you. Where is the compassion and sensitivity in that?

It's time for a change. It's time to learn what this book will teach you that it is alright to tap into the full spectrum of your feelings. And, it is time to learn when you are managing your feelings states in an unhealthy, average, or healthy way. That is why I say, "Bravo" when people are jealous, fearful, confused, sorrowful, and mad! They are feeling. It is also why I get worried when people are happy all the time because it probably means they haven't gotten the gift out of all their feelings. So get feeling! Learn how to lift them up into the healthy levels where their gifts are bestowed on you, where they can motivate you in a way that serves you, and where they help you to live great no matter what circumstances are attracted into your life.

Feelings 101

Feeling Good & Living Great

Though human beings have experienced feelings for probably about as long as they have existed perhaps only now are they coming understand them in a more in depth way. And, the more they are understood the more they can be mastered and handled well. So what exactly are feelings and how can you learn to become more sensitive to them both in yourself and others?

The idea that people could be sensitive to the feeling states of others was popularized in the public eye in the science fiction television series, *Star Trek: The Next Generation*. On the show a counselor named Deanna Troi was known for her ability to be an empathy, someone who was empathetic to the emotional states in people around her. She also role modeled the importance of sorting out and handling these feelings states well to prevent people from mishandling them or getting overwhelmed by them.

As someone who is both a counselor and empath myself, I likewise became preoccupied with learning how to handle feeling states well. And, I wanted to know how to avoid feeling overwhelmed by the barrage of feeling sensations in myself and in those around me. In many ways the teachings in this book were an attempt to master that sensitivity, especially concerning my realizations on the *anatomy of feelings* explored below.

The Anatomy of an Feeling

To begin with I believe that every feeling has three basic components: sensations, feelings, and emotions.

When examined very carefully feelings actually start out first and foremost as sensations. Later, they move into feelings. And, finally, though not always, they are expressed as emotions. Though these distinctions may seem picky they are important because the secret to managing a feeling state well is to catch it at the level of sensation, which is the level in which bodily quick automatic reactions are being produced. These reactions are a result of impact from a stimulus outside of you that creates a response within you such as through the release of hormones or bodily signals such as hairs rising on your skin. Learning to catch feelings at the level of sensation helps you rapidly and appropriately adjust to stimulus impact.

But, when you are not able to do this usually because you are "insensitive" (you sense too little) or even "overly-sensitive" (you sense too much) that adjustment at the level of sensations doesn't always happen soon enough and inhibits your ability to respond well. For example, let's say you hope to go to a ball game and suddenly someone tells you it is raining out. If you were able to respond at the level of sensation chances are you would notice a certain muscular collapse in the regions of your abdomen and chest.

That muscular reaction is most likely based upon a conditioned response cultivated either throughout your life time, or as an evolutionary response from just being a human being. If you are very aware, you will notice the change in your muscular state and be able to just simply breathe through your abdomen expanding the muscles in that region, as well as in your chest, bringing both back to equilibrium. And, at a thought and feeling level you will mostly likely shrug your shoulders and just move on in life or say something simple to yourself like, "Oh, well."

If you are not aware, and most people are not, then you will move to the next level, the level of what I am here calling the level of feeling. Now, these sensations take on coloring so to speak as they move into a feeling state. An example of six "primary colors" of feeling states used in this book are: fear, confusion, sorrow, anger, jealousy, and happiness. As sensations become feelings they are also colored by rudimentary thoughts. For example, having heard that it is raining and now you can't go to the ballgame, you may react with the feeling state of disappointment. That disappointment can still be handled fairly quickly and in a healthy way by simply acknowledging that the disappointment is present. Then, you can send yourself a simple mental message to help you deal with that disappointment quickly by telling yourself, "That's ok, I will go to a ballgame another day." Going a step further you can back up to the level of sensation and adjust your bodily reaction of a collapsed abdomen and chest.

But, often people are not able to make these kind of quick and healthy adjustments at the levels of sensation and feeling. Instead, feelings get increasingly attached to thought activating belief systems that likewise trigger emotional reactions. At times these can even result in intense emotional displays. The more intense the displays are the greater the risk that they will become unhealthy and destructive. Let's illustrate what has happened here:

1. An outside stimulus or event causes...
2. A response at the level of sensation. If not handled well it causes...
3. Feelings and rudimentary thoughts to be activated. If they are not handled well they cause...
4. Emotional reactions based on complex thoughts or beliefs to be triggered off.

Now the pickup sticks (emotions) either prevent you from feeling good and living great because your intentions are going nowhere (they are stuck), or your emotional triggers have blown everything up. The only way out is to back up and move from emotions, back to feelings, back to bodily sensations. If you have sunk down to the level of emotion this will require some thought to figure out what the belief systems (triggers) are that are setting the emotions off. And, the more thought (or story) becomes constellated around what has happened, the more thought will be required to dig yourself back out.

Because many people don't understand the differences between sensations, feelings, and emotions they tend to assume thoughts come before feelings. Yet, my own experience and observation indicate exactly the opposite. Thoughts arise increasingly as you move into feeling and emotional states in an attempt to sort them out. Now more complex interpretations or stories are created. In the case of the ballgame being cancelled because of rain you may now be inclined to say, "It's raining outside? That is awful. I really wanted to go to that game. Now my whole day is spoiled. What will I do all day long? Be bored more than likely. Great, now my whole day will suck!" Having constellated so much thought around the initial outside stimulus impact disappointment now turns into anger, which can descend into brooding or worse.

Of course thought can also be useful. Given the fact that it is raining out you could also learn to feed yourself more constructive thoughts such as the thought about going to the ballgame another day. Notice however that what is really going on here is a reduction in or simplification of thought, bringing you out of emotion, back to the feeling state, and into the level of sensation, where you can now simply breathe deeply and let the whole thing go.

This book is especially designed to teach you how to make these shifts as rapidly as possible. The secret, as you will continually see is to as much as possible stay at the level of awareness so that you can attend to outside events at the level of sensation before they become feelings at all. Shortly, you will be introduced to the master technique that helps you to do this. But, for now let's take learn more about sensations, feelings, and emotions.

Sensations. So what is a sensation? Basically it is a registration of stimuli in the environment by your nervous system, which in turn induces certain chemical reactions and bodily responses. And, as somatic (or body) psychology reveals, these sensations are usually picked up and stored in different areas of the body where different nerve groupings and glands reside. Keys to where they are being activated and stored can be found in paying attention to bodily responses such as a tingling on your skin, a tightening in your stomach, an increase in your heart rate, a change in your breathing pattern, a lump in your throat, a flush on your face, or a heightened sensation all over your body. These sensations are attempting to tell you that something is up, though typically you don't know yet what that means on a mental or emotional level. And, you don't really need to.

Why? Because as pointed out with the ballgame being cancelled, if you work with a feeling soon enough at the bodily level when it is only a sensation you can frequently manage it effectively without having to apply thought to know what it means. Using another example let's say you are at an office meeting and your boss gives you an assignment you have been hoping for to someone else. At a sensation level you notice a collapse in your chest, and again at the feeling level you experience some level of disappointment also mixed in with irritation.

What do you do now? Well, the healthiest thing to do is to simply take a few deep breaths. Why? Because dwelling on the feeling state of irritation and disappointment won't help you get the assignment back. Rather, the most rapid response is to just adjust at the level of sensation by filling up your chest again. Doing so brings back vitality in the body and also restores a certain level of confidence. In addition it brings you into a meditative state of awareness where in a more calm and peaceful space you can simply reflect on the question, "Now what?"

Feelings. And, how are feelings different from sensations? In many ways feelings color sensations by giving them a certain quality. What is coloring these sensations? Rudimentary or not very complex thoughts. When the overall pattern of your thought life is generally calm and peaceful these rudimentary thoughts will move in the direction of calm and peaceful reactions. If your rudimentary thoughts are full of triggers then your thoughts will tend to be more irrational, reactionary, and distorted.

As you learn more about the master technique you will discover that a vital key to handling your feeling states well is learning how to become the witness and to maintain mental polarization so you can clearly observe what is going on within and around you. Then from a calm place you can work with six major feeling states (fear, confusion, sorrow, anger, jealousy, and happiness), These feeling states are divided into nine different levels. The first three levels correspond to sensation and are therefore called the healthy levels. The second three levels correlate with feelings and are called the average levels. The last three levels are more emotional and reactionary and are known as the unhealthy levels. But, for now lets work with feeling states at a simple level noticing if they are "hot" and "cold."

"Hot" feelings tend towards emoting outward into the environment. When expressed in a healthy way they motivate you to take action. Expressed in an unhealthy way they emote explosively. Examples of hot feelings include anger, passion, and enthusiasm."Cold" feelings tend to move the energy of the feeling state inward. When expressed in an unhealthy way they implode (such as when they reach states of depression and despair). "Cold" feeling states used in an effective way help you "keep your cool." But, when these feeling states are repressed and cut off inappropriately they can make you "cold and indifferent." Feeling states like fear, confusion, and sorrow that have a repressed, frozen, or cloudy aspect to them often fall into this cold category. Begin then to identify feeling states in their simple form (hot/cold). Then this book will show you how to spot them in their more complex form (the nine different levels of six feeling states), so you can better maintain them at a healthy level.

Emotions. Emotions, e-mote, or move the feeling one way or the other (outward or inward). As a feeling becomes an emotion thought patterns that are more complex emerge. These complex thought patterns are comprised of belief systems that attempt to interpret or attach meaning to events. If this meaning, or story about the events, helps you to move forward in life in a positive way, then the emotion retreats back to a feeling and then back to a sensation where it is dissolved. If this meaning, or story, does not help you move forward in a positive way then it is stored as what is commonly known as a hot button or trigger.

In many ways triggers are like protective shields that cover up stored hurt and pain. In their own way they are trying to prevent you from being harmed or becoming vulnerable again. Unfortunately, when these triggers are hit they tend to launch emotional reactions that are more like explosions or implosions and are often destructive in nature. One of the reasons they are so destructive is that they are built around undigested feelings and stored sensations in the body that lack an intelligent and healthy outlet. Because they remain stored in the body and have not been fully integrated or digested in a healthy way, they act like toxins in the body that need to be discharged at some point later on

    The secret is learning how to discharge emotional triggers in a healthy way with the right amount of force and in the proper direction to minimize their destructive impact. Learning how to walk your feeling states back up from the unhealthy levels to the healthy levels using the master technique in this book will allow you to do that. After you have done so it is important to learn other coping skills apart from storing undigested emotions in such a way that they create triggers in the first place.

    For example, for a long time Jean struggled with her husband's physical and verbal abuse by imploding her feelings and getting depressed. After joining a women's support group, Jean felt strong enough to emote her hurt and anger in a forceful, but healthy way. The next time her husband starting yelling at her, cussing her out, and threatened to hit her she packed her bags and left the house. Then she refused to return unless he went into an abuser program to get the required counseling for an average of two years. Had she not been able to take such a forceful stance in a healthy way, she would have remained the victim of his aggression, which was not good for her or her children. Thus, she emoted with the right amount of force. But, if she had tried to be forceful in an aggressive way, chances are he would have also escalated and ended up abusing her even more. By learning how to be emote in a forceful way without aggression, Jean was able to increase her odds of getting healthy results.

Three Ways of Handling Feelings

Now that you are understanding the anatomy of feelings it is time to get a better overview of your specific feeling style. In general, people have three traditional responses to their feelings: they attempt to suppress or deny them (emote them in an inward way), they seek out ways to fully express them (emote them in an outward way), or they find a balanced way of handling them that knows when to skillfully submerge or express them as needed.

If your feeling style is oriented towards denying or suppressing them then you are more classically masculine in your approach. In general male culture attempts to devalue emotional display. Even boys at a young age learn to view emotions as unintelligent, sissy, baby-like, or even the enemy. Historically and even biologically there are some reasons for this. Men, especially those with high levels of testosterone, are said to have less developed limbic systems within the brain, and in many ways the limbic system is responsible for sensitivity. If you consider that for thousands of years men have been mostly responsible for hunting game and going into battle it makes sense that biologically they have less feeling awareness. That is because when in battle it is often vital to survival to be able to suppress certain feelings such as fear and remorse.

Unfortunately, this can dull feeling sensitivity, causing too many men (or women with a more masculine orientation), to become limited in their effective handling of feelings. Feelings are then viewed with disdain, denied any value, controlled, or even encouraged to become non-existent. As feelings are repressed a dry, cold, uncaring, and indifferent personality can emerge.

This "ultra-cool" style of handling feelings can be seen in movie heroes who go through incredible difficulties in life and feel no pain, regret, fear, or real joy. They become stereotypical robots frequently devoid of almost all emotional expression. Even anger becomes detached as even our hero is too cool to be angry at you, choosing instead to display that anger by ignoring and neglecting you.

Or, our hero reacts too quickly with anger that is often disproportionate in response to what set it off. For example, you make me mad, I blow off your face. Then, which is even more frightening, after exploding in violence our hero may be trained to return to an ultra calm state. Though this emotional response style may be useful for machine like men in battle, it is highly destructive in the realm of human relations. And, it is ultimately destructive to the mental, emotional, and physical health of everyone.

Another reaction to feelings is stereotypically more feminine in nature, though men may also behave in this fashion. Here, feelings are given full expression, but at the same time they often come out in an uncontrolled and hysterical manner. Much like tempests, tidal waves, and hurricanes, feelings emote with full force and intensity. It is as if they come out of nowhere to devastate and wipe you out mentally, emotionally, and even physically. Then, just as a calm state is reached, they come forth to devastate and wipe you out once again.

This kind of emotional ebb and flow is glorified in melodramas, soap operas, and cheap romance novels. All of a sudden the heroine "falls in love," is "consumed by passion," is "overwhelmed with desire." Notice the phrasing of these words. She "falls," is "consumed," or "overwhelmed." Constantly, there is the sense that something has caught her unaware. She is unable to consciously register her feeling states and has lost the ability to constructively deal with them properly.

Because she lacks so much skill in handling her emotional reactions, she may even believe that emotions are something over which she has no control. Conveniently this makes it easy for her to abdicate responsibility for her actions. After all, what could she do? She was simply ignorant, unconscious, and swept away by emotional states. Not responsible for mastering her feelings, she goes about doing whatever she pleases, at least until such emotional displays leave her exhausted, depressed, embittered, and despondent.

Feeling Good & Living Great

The third way of dealing with feelings is the balanced approach between these two extremes. Here feelings are neither repressed or overly expressed. Instead, they are shared in a way that helps you implement the lessons they are trying to teach you about how to approach life in a more healthy way. As you understand your feelings and learn to work with them in a more stable and appropriate manner, life becomes more peaceful, prosperous, and joyful. Even when you are experiencing so called negative emotions you feel good and can live great because you know how to use any feeling state to get its gift and bring about greater good in your world.

Using water as a metaphor for your feeling states you discover how to either swim in feeling waters, part the feeling waters, calm the feeling waters, or walk over them. In all of these examples, the feelings, are acknowledged, in such a way you are not overcome by them, drowning in them, or succumbing to frostbite from neglecting them. Best of all your feelings become doorways showing you how to be more fully human and even spiritual. By embracing them you embrace life allowing you to live more fully so you can make your life great overall.

Seeing Your Feeling Body

To further understand your unique feeling style you can start with a feeling analysis. Begin by examining the ways you experience feelings. This requires the capacity to objectively witness yourself, a process that will be described a little later in this book, and one that is also discussed in more detail in my *Meditation: The Path for Peace* book. For now just begin by answering some of these questions. What are your thoughts about feelings in general? Are there certain feelings which are easier for you to express than others (such as happiness, anger, fear, sorrow, and so forth)? How do you relate to feelings? Do you try to cut them off or freeze them? Do you prefer to express them? Can you do this appropriately?

Next, see if you can get a better understanding of your relationship to your feelings by using water as a metaphor. For example, let's use the metaphor of an ocean. Do your feelings have a peaceful ebb and flow? Or, are they filled with large, erratic tidal waves crashing into the sand? Maybe they are like a stormy brooding sea keeping others wary of you? Or, are they friendly and supportive to the "ships" which try to cross over them?

Maybe your feelings relate to other metaphors using water. Maybe they are more like a gentle, nourishing rain or a gloomy and threatening thunderstorm. Maybe they babble cheerily like a brook or steam over like a teapot. Perhaps, they are similar to a calm, clear lake or a foggy, dark swamp. Or, you may have calm areas with whirlpools in a few spots here and there. Fog or clouds may also be present, especially in relation to parts which are confused and unclear.

Finally, there may be such a lack of feeling that all that exists is a dry lake, an arid desert, or a frozen tundra. Often this happens when a long period of time has gone by without love, nourishment, or support from others. Or, instead of drying up your feelings, you may try to cut them off or freeze them. If so, notice if your frozen feeling resemble an area around the north or south pole where the land mass is entirely frozen. Or, are they more like patches of ice blocks floating in open water?

Regarding the ice blocks you might consider are they are mostly invisible or visible? That is, can other people see you have frozen feeling patches right away, or do they only find out when they hit them, much as the Titanic hit an unseen iceberg and was submerged? Simply note whatever images you respond to as a means to help you relate to and identify your general feeling state.

Using these water symbols you can even take a piece of paper and draw a picture of your emotional body. As you do so be careful not to censor what you are drawing. It is best not to have a preconceived idea like "I'm going to draw an ocean." Just reflect on your feelings in general and let whatever images that come to mind be reflected onto the paper. Create as many drawings as you wish, reflecting on the variety of feeling states you experience in yourself while a part of different environmental settings. You may even wish to keep a journal of your drawings doing one a week or a month for a sustained period of time.

The Role of the Witness

Feeling Good & Living Great

So how do you begin to master your feeling states? As previously stated the most important step is to train yourself to quickly register and work more effectively with sensations. But, this can only be done as you become increasingly perceptive, awake, and sensitive in a healthy way. How do you this? By learning how to be more aware of what is going on around and within you, especially as it impacts your body. For example, maybe you enter a room full of people and as you do so you find yourself feeling queasy, anxious, and uncertain in your stomach area. Or, you may feel warm and excited in your heart region. You may even find yourself stimulated in your genital area, or focusing upwards around your head.

All of these signals are attempting to make you aware early on what may be taking place within and around you. Knowing this you can either relax and dissolve the sensation at a bodily level, or you can bring in thought and attempt to see more clearly what is up. In this way you can gain insight into how to feel and act in a healthy and appropriate way.

The other method is to pay attention to what is going on in another person's body at a sensorial level. This includes being able to read facial expressions and other bodily cues. In fact, a lot of what passes for psychic sensitivity is really a psychological ability to read body language in others well. The point is the more you can sense what is going on in the other person the more you will be able to work with the feeling states of others in an effective way.

Dr. Lisa Love

Cultivating the Witness

Of course getting to the point where you can observe sensations sooner and at a more healthy level usually only happens as you learn to work with feeling states more effectively. And, it only occurs as you learn to clear up and lift out of heavy emotional states that may be preventing you from sensing things soon enough and in the right way. Though there are many methods to master various feeling states and recover from heavy emotional ones (and this book lists over thirty), the first step is to learn how to cultivate the witness or observer. What is the witness? It is that part of you that helps you see and observe reality more clearly and in an impartial way.

Whether you know it or not you have probably already called upon that witness or impartial observer many times in your life. Whenever you attempt to answer questions to get insight into yourself, the witness is being utilized. You also are calling upon your witness whenever you set the intention to step outside your own point of view and consider another way of looking at or thinking about something. When emotional triggers are going off, the act of simply noticing that you are triggering activates the witness. And, you reinforce that witness by saying to yourself mentally, "Oh, I'm triggering, what is this about?"

Still, it is not enough to just occasionally call upon the witness in yourself. You must cultivate it so that you can call upon it rapidly whenever you find yourself in an emotional state. That is why meditation practices (such as those found in my *Meditation: The Path for Peace* book) and something known as the "disidentification exercise" are essential. Both help you increasingly become the witness, or enter into the attitude of the observer, on a more reliable basis.

What is meant by a disidentification exercise? Basically, it relates to your identity, or who you believe yourself to be. For example, how do you answer when someone asks you the question, "Who are you?" Do you answer according to what you do for a living? (I'm a writer, counselor, accountant, programmer, etc.). Do you answer based upon your strengths or weaknesses? (I'm a hard working person. I'm a talented artist. I'm an addict. I'm a loser). Or, do you answer according to your social position? (I'm rich, poor, middle class, popular, unpopular). Maybe you even answer according to your belief systems (I'm a Christian, Jew, Muslim, Hindu, Buddhist, Republican, Democrat, Independent, etc.)

All these statements of identity are important because they reveal some level of who you believe yourself to be. But, here is the difficulty, these statements of identity can also seriously limit the reality of the sum total of who you really are. That's why when you say something to yourself like, "Oh, well, that is just the way I am," regarding a negative behavior pattern, what you are really saying is that you are trapped within that identity, that particular pattern, and have decided that it is impossible to change. In a way you are right, it is impossible unless you free yourself from the cage of this identity. That is why you need to "dis-identify" from whatever it is you want to change, and learn instead to identify with something on a higher level that gives you the power to make the necessary shifts.

If you cannot do this you will be limited to what you attach your identity to because you will have *become* the problem or limitation. That means you can no longer *manage* it! People who cannot heal and become victims after they have been traumatized by someone face this challenge. For example, When *I am* the problem (meaning I have identified with it), it reinforces my sense of helplessness so I can not *do* anything about it. I *become* a sick person, instead of someone learning to manage a disease. I *become* a cripple instead of someone with a disability. I *become* an alcoholic instead of someone who has a drinking problem. I *become* an emotional cripple or tyrant, instead of someone who needs to learn how to observe and work with various feeling states in a better way.

Therefore, in order to change any behavior in the long run, it is important to acknowledge that you *have* a problem, while at the same time learning how to dis-identify with *being* the problem. Maybe that is why famous scientist Albert Einstein said that, "The significant problems we have cannot be solved at the same level of thinking with which we created them." So, if you are not the problem, who are you really? Essentially you are *a spiritual being* having a human experience. And, that human experience involves managing and working with various problems. Therefore, when you are a spiritual being you are coming from a higher level and will be better able to manage a disease, deal with a drinking problem, cope with a disability, or handle various feelings states well. Having shared this new notion of who you really are let's learn the disidentification exercise.

Disidentification Exercise.

1. Sit in a comfortable chair, or in a supportive cross legged position on the floor.
2. Start to observe your breathing. Simply allow yourself to breath deeply in and out a few times, then allow your breathing to settle into a natural rhythm.
3. Now turn your attention to your physical body. Spend time observing all its various parts and functions. Then say softly to yourself, "I have a body, but I am *not* my body. I am not this (pain, anxiety, or whatever else emerges physically as you go through this meditation). I am *the witness* of my physical form."
4. Next, turn your attention to your emotional nature. Consider all the various feelings you experience day in and day out. Then say softly to yourself., "I have emotions, but I am *not* my emotions. I am not this (upset, anger, fear, depression or whatever else happens to emerge emotionally during this meditation). I am *the witness* of my emotional states."
5. Moving on, turn your attention to your mind. Consider your ability to observe all the various

thoughts coming and going. Say to yourself softly, "I have a mind, but I am *not* my mind. I am not this (mental chatter, distraction, negativity, or whatever is arising during this meditation). I am *the witness* of my mental states."

6. Note that because you have the ability to observe your physical body, emotions, and mind that alone indicates that you are indeed the witness of these things.
7. Then affirm. "I am the witness of my life." Note any thoughts, feelings, physical reactions, and sensations which happen in response to this.
8. If possible go one step further and ask, "Who is the witness?" Answer, "I am Spirit, the soul, a spiritual being having this human experience."
9. Close the exercise and record your experiences.

The advantage of practicing this exercise on a regular basis is that as you disidentify from your thoughts, emotions, and bodily responses, and identify as the witness (Spirit or soul), you will be better able to call upon your identity as the witness (Spirit or soul) as needed. You can even dress rehearse being the witness (Spirit or soul) by reviewing emotionally tense situations you have experienced in the past. Then go over them again this time imagining that you are handling them in a more calm way using the witness (Spirit or soul) to guide you. You can also do the same for events that might happen in the future making it more likely you will act in a manner that is more calm, soulful, poised, and peaceful.

Feeling Good & Living Great

Mental Polarization

One of the additional benefits of cultivating the witness and learning to disidentify is that of achieving mental polarization. What is mental polarization? It is the capacity to no longer be driven by emotional impulse, but by reason. Reason is not simply a process of learning how to be objective. The capacity to reason is much more than a cold logical process of observation and analysis. It is actually a state of love in the mind helping you access all levels of the mind so you can direct your feeling states with greater skill and wisdom.

When you have love in the mind reason gives you insight into what is going on in you, in others, and in everything around you. Reason allows you to cultivate understanding. It gives you a sense of connection and compassion with everything and everyone around you including yourself. And, reason gives you a greater capacity for empathy and love

If reason and mental polarization are so important why do so many people struggle with both? Mainly because human beings live out of a state of *kama-manas* or desire (kama) mind (manas). A desire filled mind is really an impulsive and emotionally laden mind. When you constantly act in an impulsive way it typically means you are failing to reason things out, or really think things through. Because of this failure you are more likely to suffer the consequences of impulsive and misguided behaviors.

People who live from a state of *kama-manas* are

also unable to think critically and objectively. And, they tend to be more egotistical, selfish, and incapable of seeing the larger picture or whole. Looked at carefully even if they claim to be logical and objective, they are not truly reasonable, since reason connects them to a greater whole. That is why they can do whatever they want to selfishly indulge their own desires, and may be very logical and objective about their ability to do so, yet be acting irrationally from a larger point of view.

What is happening in regards to global warming is an example of this. In an attempt to remain within a certain comfort zone, or to protect their vested interests, people "logically" and "objectively" defend and protect their habit patterns and vested interests, even if in the bigger picture they are destroying the very environment that sustains them. Ultimately kama-manasic people are then disconnected from a bigger picture, which can lead to destruction, decay, and overall unhappiness in life.

To rise above *kama-manas* it is important not only to think, but to love. Only then can you truly reason or be truly reasonable. Only then can you become mentally polarized. Only then can compassion and a mental realization of at-one-ment bring about a sense of responsibility for using the mind to help master various feeling states, so that your love for self and others is expanded and not submerged.

For an even better understanding of what mental polarization looks like let's consider the following list of specific points..

Feeling Good & Living Great

Mental polarization produces the ability to:

1. See both sides of an issue.
2. Calmly and rationally observe and inquire.
3. Understand the meaning or reason of what is before you.
4. See cause and effect or the consequences of certain causes you put into effect.
5. Use cause to produce harmonious and loving results.
6. Consciously decide what you will think, and as you think decide to do so along lines that produce greater harmony, compassion, and peace.
7. Create ideals not based on desire, or just for the good of oneself, but for the good of the whole.

Mental polarization also means that you have learned to access not just the lower levels of mind, but the higher levels. The lower levels are mostly reactive, impulsive, selfish and desire filled. The higher levels allow for more objectivity and critical thinking skills. And. understanding, compassion, insight, and reason are produced. Let's get a greater understanding of these.

Thinking It Over

Feeling Good & Living Great

On the way to mental polarization and cultivating the witness and mental polarization it is important to understand four levels of mind and how to utilize each in a positive way so you can feel good and live great. And, it is necessary to learn when you are operating at a level of mind that is not serving you so you can shift to another level to cope better with your feeling states. In general the four levels of mind are: the instinctual mind, the motivational mind, the logical mind, and the intuitive mind.

The Instinctual Mind

The instinctual mind is the most basic level of mind. It is based upon long term conditioning and has its roots in the most ancient part of the brain. On a positive level these instincts help you to know how to respond effectively to your environment (quickly dodge away from a ball about to hit you, take your hand immediately away from a hot stove). For this reason the instinctual mind is reflexive. When working well it reacts quickly and effectively to help you.

When not working well the instinctual mind becomes more reactive versus reflexive. Now, you don't just quickly get out of the way of the oncoming ball or remove your hand from the hot stove; you cuss and swear at the ball or the stove and make a big scene about how you almost got hit or burned. Of course not all reaction is unhealthy. Some of it can be natural and human. It just becomes unhealthy when your reaction becomes overly emotional and excessive. Then it no longer serves you and can even harm you.

Many people also confuse the instinctual mind's reflexive capacity with insight. That is why people are heard to say that you should "think with your gut" or "listen to what your gut says." What people don't understand is that these gut sensations come from a level of mind that doesn't help give an overview or allows for fresh insights. Rather, the instinctual mind only gives you a summary of what your previous experiences have taught you or what you have already assimilated and digested.

Because few people understand how the gut is based upon the past they often confuse intuition with instinctual impulses. But, the intuitive mind and instinctual minds are not the same. The intuitive mind always reveals something new. And, intuitions have nothing to do with hunches or reflexive impulses like the decision to go left or right. Rather, the intuitive mind is at a higher level of functioning than the instinctual mind and unless you understand this you won't learn how to cultivate the witness, become mentally polarized, or handle your feeling states in a healthy manner. That is because the intuitive mind has to be engaged for you to do these things. When it is not and you are only acting from your instinctual mind you are actually living in a fairly primitive state.

If you think about it, when you come from the level of your instincts (or gut), you are really coming from the region of your stomach and digestive organs. These organs help you process what you have already taken in, so you can digest what you have experienced and discern what is worth keeping and then eliminate the rest. That is what reflexive or "gut thinking" is about. If your life lessons have been learned in a positive way then your instinctual mind gives you healthy reflexes on a physical and emotional level and is serving you. But, if you have not fully digested or learned these lessons then listening to your gut may not be good for you.

That is because these gut responses are more reactive than reflexive and are based upon reactive emotional hot buttons or triggers. As has been shared triggers come about due to an unhealthy digestion of past experiences. Because the lessons of the past have not been assimilated in a way that really serves you, they do not get eliminated from your thinking. Instead, they get stored and in many ways clog up and congest your thinking and feeling states.

Why then do so many people sing the praises of trusting their guts? One reason is because when you are using your instinctual mind well, it informs you about how to assimilate or digest the experiences you are confronted with in a healthy way. A healthy gut response is literally a bodily response that lets you know if an action you are about to pursue is something you should really assimilate (or engage in) in the first place.

I am reminded of a client of mine whose husband was offered a job that would move his family from New York to California. It was an amazing opportunity with a well-known company. But, on the flight to California to interview with the company a second time and consider accepting the offer, my client noticed that he felt a queasy sensation in his gut from the time the plane took off throughout the entire flight. At one point he even had to go and use the restroom where he promptly threw up. Instead of considering what might be causing him to feel so upset, he discounted the signals of his instinctual mind, and used his motivational mind to talk himself into moving forward because everything looked so idyllic and seemed to what he had been looking for career wise.

At first when his family made the move to the San Francisco Bay area from New York state he was thrilled. He rented a beautiful home for his family by the water and threw himself into his work to prove his value to the company. Then three months later his company announced that it had been bought out by a larger company and as part of the merge with the new company it laid off a number of its employees. Naturally, those who were most recently hired were the first to go including him.

Out of work he was mortified by the fact that he had left a secure job and moved his family all the way across country only to end up unemployed. Though he found another job in the San Francisco Bay area after four months of unemployment, he felt battered and bruised. This sense of shame was made worse when months later he discovered that the company that had originally hired him had known lay offs might happen after the merger was finalized, but had ignored revealing this fact to anyone because they wanted to hire new employees during the buy-out to sweeten the deal. Of course my client was not really responsible for that, but looking back he did tell me that clues were there and he had ignored them.

He even told me that he now understood he could have avoided a lot of pain if he had paid more attention to his instinctual mind or gut and acknowledged the signals that were telling him that despite outer appearances something was very unsettling about the offer. He even kicked himself for having ignored some sound logical advice a co-worker had shared with him on how to protect himself and his family before he accepted the final offer. His friend had said, "If they want you that badly, then ask them to give you a guarantee in the contract that you will be employed for two years. If they break the contract before that time is up then require them to give you a certain amount of money to buy you out of it."

Regrettably, like so many people hurt during both the dot-com and housing market crises, my client had not paid attention to his instinctual mind and it's warnings that he might be risking too much and be getting involved in something he and his family couldn't fully handle. In a real way he was ignoring what he was sensing and feeling and attempting to over-ride it. He also failed to be mentally polarized, which uses all four levels of the mind and gets a healthy overview of everything. Instead, he allowed his motivational mind (based upon hopes, wishes, and desires) and impulsive feelings to over-ride everything else in a way that helped him feel temporarily good about what he was doing, but in the long run caused him to neither feel good or live great at all.

So, when and how is it important to listen to your instinctual mind and what it is trying to tell you? Especially during the action phase of any change it's important to consider signals that your instinctual mind might be sending you. Ways to build a more powerful and effective instinctual mind include taking time to fully digest and learn from your past experiences so you can train yourself in the future to *act* versus react in a more positive and effective manner. Insight therapy is another tool that can help you work through triggers residing within the instinctual mind so you can better digest and reframe those triggers and blocks into healthier thought patterns and belief systems that will help you act and react more effectively. So will learning to use the techniques and teachings throughout this book.

Other ways to cultivate the instinctual mind include certain types of body awareness techniques like yoga, martial arts, breathing techniques, dance, and somatic psychology training. These methods are helpful because they allow you to more readily recognize and inquire into what is going on within not only your gut regions, but all regions of your body. And, they help you understand what those body signals are trying to communicate to you so you can act upon them appropriately.

Questions to Develop the Instinctual Mind

- What instinctual habit patterns are serving my life the most so that I cultivate better reflexive habits?

- What instinctual habit patterns need changing because they cause too many triggers?
- What lessons do I need to digest, learn from, and change to improve the quality of my life?

The Motivational Mind

One step above the instinctual mind is the motivational mind, which is the aspect of mind that is the most kama-manasic in nature. Here the mind is driven by desires and emotions. At the unhealthy levels it is addictive, obsessive, impulsive, and defensive. At the healthy levels it provides motivation and drive giving you the energy and persistence you need to evolve and change your life for the better.

At the unhealthy levels the heavy emotional and impulsive nature of the motivational mind prevents you from seeing people and events clearly making feeling states more difficult to manage (especially without the witness in place to help you understand what is going on with your feelings states). Coming from this level of mind alone feeling states are more likely to implode and cause you to self-destruct, or explode creating difficulties with others.

In many ways you begin to look like a person with buttons, or triggers, all over the place making you far too sensitive and often way too irrational. People may frequently find that they have to be very careful around you lest your triggers get accidently hit and you implode or explode. When those triggers are hit, your motivation is to deny them or defend them, versus get insight into them. In a very real way you are unreasonable because your emotional reactions make you difficult to reason with.

These out of control emotional reactions may also cause you to resort to addictive patterns as a means to try to control and manage them. Smoking, drinking, drugs, sex, thrill seeking — anything to keep you deflected from a true understanding of what you are really feeling. And, though these addictive behaviors might make you feel good temporarily, ultimately they do not lead *to the* good and what is good for you. For this reason they do not help you lead a great life in the long run.

At the healthier levels the motivational mind draws you towards a desire to liberate yourself from defensive and reactive emotional states. It provides the fuel you need to release yourself from destructive habits so you can move into healthier ways of being. Deeply wanting to be freed from pain you use your motivational mind to propel you towards becoming the observer so you can see clearly what you need to do to change. Then, like sticky glue, this aspect of mind can give you the patience and persistence you need to make these changes become lasting every day of your life.

Tools that help at this level (apart from knowing how to become the observer and manage your feeling states well), include many classic law of attraction tools such as affirmations, vision boards, and visualizations.

Feeling Good & Living Great

These tools are very helpful because they allow you to dress rehearse something so you can experience it as if it was real. The more real it feels the more you will be likely to make it a reality because you will be putting in the effort to make it true. Setting an intention is another useful motivational mind tool. Intentions help you get clear about what you want and set your will into motion helping to ensure that your desires will be met.

Keeping your mind in a positive state is also helpful. You are much more likely to be motivated when you believe you can really make something happen the way you want it to. By seeing the glass as half full instead of half empty you increase the odds that you can motivate yourself to move forward in a positive way. The glass half full technique also helps you stay open to higher levels of your mind when things don't go the way you believe they should, because as you access those higher levels of mind you are more inclined to believe that with the right tools and insights things can and will get better. Without being able to look on the positive side of things you may shut down and not see how every so called failure may really be just a means of teaching you the lessens you need to learn so you improve yourself overall.

Questions to Develop the Motivational Mind

- What exactly is best for me to want now in my life?
- How much do I really want it and what will help me want it more?

- What am I willing to change to help me get it, and what must I change to ensure I can attract it to me?

The Logical Mind

The logical mind in many ways is where the witness and observer state begins. On a very practical level the logical mind gives you the capacity to put your thoughts in order so you can see the cause and effect of events in your life. As mentioned before discerning cause and effect is part of the process of developing mental polarization. In many ways the logical mind is like a computer that operates on an "if—then" principle. If I do A, B, C and D, then it will very likely lead to E, F, and G.

That is why the logical mind is a specialist. It knows a lot about a little. Instead of working to get an overview in a flash (which is what the intuitive mind allows you to do), the logical mind encourages you to learn specific steps that get you to where you want to go. And, the odds of getting there are higher because the logical mind is careful to avoid the problems of the lower two levels of mind that include instinct, impulse, luck, or wishful thinking that are less likely to help you really manifest results. Instead, the logical mind is more scientific looking for reliability and predictability helping you actually achieve what you want (and what Spirit wants for you) because you have a reasonable amount of certainty that what you say and do has the power to produce specific results, and will produce them over and over again.

Feeling Good & Living Great

In contrast, the motivational mind can prevent you from being logical because it operates mostly out of enthusiasm. It wants to rush ahead to get what you want no matter what the odds or even the costs. When you operate only from the motivational mind you are less likely to think carefully or consider the best strategy for getting to where you want to go. And, when you fail to get what you want feeling states like anger, sorrow, jealousy, confusion, fear, and misguided happiness will all emerge making you seemingly emotionally out of control.

The logical mind counters these problems because it helps you organize and systematize your thoughts, manage your feeling states more objectively, and helps you create a strategic plan to get to where you need to go. Strategic plans consist of specific steps you need to follow in order to produce specific results. By breaking these steps into small manageable bites you are less likely to feel overwhelmed (an aspect of confusion), angry, depressed, fearful, and so forth.

Often I use strategic plans when I coach people. For example, when I teach clients how to lose weight I usually start them out by telling them to just go to the gym and sit in the parking lot. At first they think this is silly. Then they discover that just the act of getting dressed and sitting in the parking lot gets them motivated to at least think about working out. Next, I encourage them to go inside the gym and look around.

Then I invite them to get a gym membership. Eventually, they learn to go inside and do something easy like walk ten minutes on the treadmill or swim a couple laps in the pool. Eventually, ten minutes on the treadmill turns into twenty minutes or more. A couple laps in the pool moves up to thirty. Before they know it one day at the gym became three days or more of participating in twenty to thirty minutes of aerobic exercise. These baby steps increase the likelihood of them not sabotaging themselves because they feel wiped out by having set goals that were too big to start with.

Other great logical mind tools include things like creating mind maps, setting up daily priorities and goals that you can follow through on, establishing agendas, and keeping daily logs and journals of your intentions in the morning and afternoon. In regards to feeling good and living great a strategic plan (such as the master plan for managing your emotions given throughout this book) helps you manage various feeling states better as well. By pulling out that plan whenever you find yourself falling apart, you enable yourself to reside more within your logical mind and are better able to use your witness to help you get the gift out of your feelings so they help instead of hinder your life.

Cultivating the Logical Mind

- What steps do I need to take to increase the odds that I can achieve what I want and what Spirit wants for me?
- What are my priorities at this point in my life and what should they be at this time?

Feeling Good & Living Great

- How can I rearrange my priorities to attract a life of greater joy and bliss?

The Intuitive Mind

Though you can manage your feeling states fairly effectively with just the logical mind, the logical mind alone cannot help you get to the highest levels where you go beyond facts and procedures and become truly uplifted, enlightened, and inspired. That is where the intuitive mind comes into play, because it puts you more directly in touch with your soul. From there you can get a more holistic, comprehensive, inclusive and clear view of your life and its difficulties. And, you can access real solutions to your problems, which are much more likely to come in a flash bringing not only insight, but relief from mental and emotional strain.

Because the intuition does not incline you to solutions that are impulsive and represent quick fixes, when you listen to your intuitive mind you tend to attract more of what you need for the highest good of yourself and others. And, you are more inclined to make healthier choices for yourself, allowing you to feel better about who you are and how you live your life no matter what the outer conditions you are faced with.

One of the best methods for getting in touch with the intuitive mind is through the practice of meditation. No surprise then that research done by Dr. Richard Davidson of the University of Wisconsin showed people who regularly meditate have significantly better moral reasoning, happiness, and other positive emotional states. Why? Because meditation stimulates the prefrontal cortex, the part of the brain associated with these qualities. Plus, meditation helps you quiet the mind allowing you to access the intuition. And, it brings about greater mental stability helping you to become mentally polarized.

The intuition brings about fresh insights, or those "ah-ha" moments that help you find a way through the labyrinth of life. That's why people who are highly intuitive are often considered to be geniuses since they "genesis" or give birth to new ideas, inventions, and approaches that either they, or even the entire human race, have not thought about before. The intuition can also send you preventive signals that will prompt you to avoid what may end up being a difficult road ahead.

So how do you keep your intuitive mind open? As mentioned meditation is the best way. So is keeping your body chemistry and biology healthy by living a lifestyle that allows your brain chemistry to function well. Prayer also helps, especially if after making a prayer request you are listening for an answer from the Divine. Whatever the method, stay open to fresh insights regarding how to move beyond any difficult space you find yourself in. Let your intuitive mind help you move out of rigid ways of thinking into something fresh, positive, and liberating. Allow it to show you how to handle both your thoughts and feelings in a more constructive way. Then insights can emerge regarding practical steps you may need to take to improve

Feeling Good & Living Great

your health, finances, relationships, career, and your overall approach to life.

Cultivating the Intuitive Mind

- What does Spirit want for me to attract in my life?
- What will help me increase my daily quota of joy?
- What insights can help me breakthrough limitations in my mind, emotions, and actions that stop me from living a life of joy and prosperity?

Handling Feelings Well

Feeling Good & Living Great

If you are not fully adept at working with a feeling when it is mainly at the level of sensation, then learning how to work with a greater range of feeling states is very useful. In the upcoming chapters you will be exposed to fifty-four feeling states with six major groupings of feelings divided into nine levels. You will also learn how to identify the intensity of these different feeling states so you can see if you are working with a feeling in a healthy, average, or unhealthy way. But, for now let's get a better understanding of working with feelings in general.

Working With Specific Feeling States

To begin with the six major groupings of feeling states listed in this book include: fear, confusion, sorrow, anger, jealousy, and happiness. With each of these six major groupings review how you handle each one in general. For example, let's start with anger. Begin by noticing your overall beliefs about anger and how comfortable or uncomfortable you are with it. Do you believe you should never get angry? Does anger frighten you? Do you get angry easily? Does anger have any value? As you answer these questions lift into the witness or observer part of yourself to discover why you believe as you do.

Maybe you discover that you recoil from anger and believe it has no value. Maybe that belief is due to a religious teaching. Or, maybe you recoil because you are afraid of your anger, both in yourself and others. That's how Jenny felt. Growing up in a household where her parents were frequently shouting, and where both parents had explosive styles of anger that resulted in frequent emotional belittlement and abuse of each other and Jenny as well, she came to believe that anger in any form was wrong.

Ironically, in many ways Jenny was angry at anger. She hated what it had done to her family and her life. Because Jenny had never been exposed to the gifts of anger, she could only believe that anger was bad. Since every feeling can be positive if used well, Jenny was unable to derive any of the healthy benefits from anger, since she had only ever experienced the negative ones. Now because she did not know how to use her anger as a tool for self-preservation and protection, or how to transform her anger into energy, Jenny often found herself in a different emotional state other than anger, most commonly anxiety and depression.

True, her anxiety helped to diffuse her anger for the moment, but it also kept her in a state of perpetual ambivalence, worry and fear. Trapped in these feeling states she was never able to free herself from negative circumstances. She simply learned to tolerate them, going numb to herself, others, and life in the process.

Over time the end result was a chronic state of depression. Metaphorically, I often speak of depression as a swamp. It is a mixture of unresolved grief and unexpressed anger. As this grief is buried and the anger is stuffed, an attitude of toxic helpless-ness emerges. Issues in life just sit there unresolved giving you the belief that you have no other choice but to go through life with a chronic sense of dissatisfaction, waiting, longing, frustration, and pain.

Of course, your experience of anger may be more like Paul's. Raised by both a physically and verbally abusive father, Paul at last found the power as a teenager to give his father a taste of his own medicine. Having beat up his father to the point of nearly putting him in the hospital, Paul was surprised at how satisfied he felt. Finally, he was free of the constant physical abuse he had experienced most of his life. He learned something significant, his anger gave him power. And, he used that anger in a powerful way when he joined the military and left for Iraq.

But, Paul also discovered that as he himself became increasingly explosive with his anger, he was growing more and more into the likeness of his father. When he first came to see me for counseling, he had left the military and was now a medical response nurse working on an E.R. unit. He was struggling to redirect his anger into something constructive. Yet, in his personal life he was dismayed to find himself getting verbally abusive with his own anger. Then in a fight with his girlfriend, he even broke a glass window he was so upset. In fear, she left him. His initial response was to use his anger to plot out an act of revenge on her for having abandoned him. Fortunately, he called me instead and we began the process of helping him heal his anger. And, over time I taught him methods for expressing anger in a more healthy way.

In both these examples, neither Jenny or Paul used

their anger in a positive way. Fortunately, in this book you will learn what I call the gifts of anger (along with the gifts of five major emotional states) so that anger can have a positive benefit. But, for now take the time to consider your relationship to anger. Then review the other feeling states (confusion, sorrow, anger, jealousy, and happiness) and how you relate to them. If need be get out a journal or notebook and write your understanding down.

Notice with each feeling state if you avoid or cultivate it. Discover how comfortable you are with each one. What triggers are set off by each? How much conscious control do you have when dealing with various feelings? What are your belief systems about them? In other words, what were you taught about the proper way to feel and express emotions? After a thorough review consider what your ideal expression of each feeling would be like. Then, make a commitment to achieve a more balanced relationship with each feeling state you review.

When Feelings Become Emotions

Ideally, when feelings become emotions they are emoted or expressed with the minimal expenditure of motion, or emotional force. Then a sense of overall calm, harmony, or well-being is present allowing you to handle the emotion with the least amount of wear and tear on your overall being or on the being of another person. But, at times you may need to become deliberately more forceful if a a situation demands it. Usually, this happens when you are confronted with the aggressive energy of another, forcing you to defend yourself for your own safety and well being.

At the same time, the quality of the force should remain high even though the degree of force may be large. High quality force retains a sense of compassion, respect, and clarity in the interaction even if you are emotionally forceful in the situation. In many ways it is like making a clean cut during surgery allowing for the least amount of pain and the maximum amount of healing.

Tim knew how to do this when he ended his engagement with Suzette. They had been engaged for two years, but when Suzette moved to another state to pursue her college degree, Tim found the distance between them too difficult. Though he cared a great deal for Suzette, after one year of attempting to keep the relationship going he knew he couldn't manage that amount of distance for three more years. So, one day when Suzette flew in to meet him, he respectfully, but clearly and directly told her their engagement was over. Naturally, Suzette was hurt, but Tim made it a point to never waver in his resolve even when for the next few months Suzette begged him to reconsider. The result? Suzette reported to me in a counseling session that she had never healed so fast from a breakup in her entire life. The reason she stated was totally because Tim was forceful, clear, compassionate, and consistent in his use of emotional force.

Unfortunately, when the quality of the force is low and the degree of force is high, then the results are usually damaging. Abuse is often an example of this. Compassion, respect, and clarity do not exist, and when combined with intense emotional force people often say and do things they regret, harming themselves and others in the process. Sadly, our society is experiencing more and more of this even glorifying it in verbal "discussions" where people attempt to shout each other down, producing a lot of emotional heat, but no light in terms of how best to resolve difficulties effectively. Thus, problems are never resolved. They are simply buried through emotional intensity until they cycle back up when emotional tension builds up again, resulting in yet another blow out of emotional force.

Likewise, when the quality of force is low and the degree of force is low, you end up being weak and ineffective in your emotional interactions. Then you are subject to the abuse, neglect, and disrespect of others, leaving you prone to states of confusion and depression as your self-esteem slowly withers, and you even start to act as if abuse and neglect are a normal part of life.

Mary had this happen to her chronically over time. For many years her husband was verbally abusive and accustomed to getting his way in the home. He would even do many things to disrespect her like having multiple affairs that Mary knew of, but was afraid due to her financially and emotional dependency to confront. Occasionally, Mary would attempt to convey her dissatisfaction. But, Mary did so without any power or conviction. For this reason her husband knew she would never follow through and act upon her discontent; therefore, Mary's hurt and anger were easily dismissed.

Weak and ineffectual emotional displays are useless then unless done with the right amount of force so that there is power in a statement, and with the right amount of quality so there is harmlessness. Civil rights movements such as those led by Martin Luther King Jr, and Gandhi where non-violent resistance were the keys are examples of the right use of emotional force.

Without this kind of emotional display, you are not mobilized into action in the right way. Then your thoughts and intentions do not become reality in your life. The "pickup sticks" of feelings and emotions are not removed either because you fail to try to remove them at all, or you fail to remove them in the right way. Having handled your feeling states and emotions poorly you may even create unintended and possibly even destructive results. Fortunately, as you learn to register emotions soon enough at the level of sensation or feeling these destructive results will be less likely. But, even then if you slip into emotional display you can still get positive results if you can learn to emote in a highly constructive way.

Working with Emotional Triggers

As mentioned when feelings are not handled well they turn into emotions where they can be stored as triggers, waiting like land mines to be set off as soon as someone accidently stumbles upon them. How do triggers develop? As indicated before when a feeling state becomes an emotion it is because an increased level of thought manifesting in assumptions, expectations, and interpretation is coming into play. Eventually those thoughts crystallize into beliefs, which are habit patterns of thought regarding your perceptions of how the world is, or should be.

As a reminder at the level of sensation there is little to no thought. You are simply in the state of witnessing what is going on. For example, you see a needle heading towards your skin. The needle enters your skin. You experience a sharp sensation. The needle leaves and the sharp sensation is gone. The experience ends and you move on. As feeling enters in so does thought with the tendency to give meaning, or interpretation, to events. Usually the interpretation is kept fairly simple at such as something being "good or bad."

Now, the sharp sensation is experienced as pain, and that pain is felt as bad. Because the needle is viewed as having delivered the pain, a feeling emerges that the needle is also bad. As the intensity of the feeling increases it gets heavier and becomes an emotion. At the same time as more thought enters in a belief system is created. For example, now that I know that needles and pain are bad, I believe I must avoid and resist pain, and perhaps needles altogether.

But, pain can at times lead to growth, and though a needle may deliver a temporary sensation of pain, it can also help prevent more pain in the long run, such as preventing a disease that would spread if you did not get the remedy to help prevent or stop it through the instrument of the needle. The secret is to as much as possible lift out of the emotional reaction, cultivate a more detached awareness (again known as the witness), and move the emotion back up to the realm of sensation where the emotional impact is diffused and replaced by a sense of well being.

Too often, the emotion remains stuck (akin to the pickup sticks in the *Kerplunk* game), primarily because the beliefs that have been attached to them are unhealthy. They lead you downward into the realm of increased fear, confusion, sorrow, anger, jealousy, and misguided ways of obtaining happiness. They do not lead you upward into love, clarity, compassion, energy, fulfillment, and joy. The more unhealthy and unrealistic your belief about yourself, people, and life the more they cluster into emotional triggers, waiting in hiding for release, waiting for something or someone to free them by setting them off.

In counseling Jean became aware of one of her major emotional triggers. It was related to a crucial point in her life where she needed the support of her husband, but had not received it. Acting as a dutiful wife, she had given up a career opportunity to help her husband advance in his career over time. His did, and as his income and opportunities accelerated, she found herself growing more and more dependent on him. At the same time she became more and more resentful.

And, she felt increasingly isolated, powerless and worthless as she was forced to rely on his income for support. Confused about how to deal with her growing helplessness and anger, she tried to just remain positive. But, despite her best efforts along these lines, whenever her husband would come home with a new bonus, promotion, or job opportunity, she found herself increasingly unable to stop the tears from flowing, or to keep her anger from erupting.

Emotional triggers are like this. Whether you want them to or not when a trigger (or button) is pushed, the energy stored up around that trigger goes into motion frequently resulting in an unhealthy display of emotion. And, though it feels good at the time (because the build up of tension around the trigger is released), the end result is like walking through a mine field. As those mines explode your self-respect may be damaged, your health may be injured delivering high blood pressure for example), your relationships may be dismantled, and instead of living great, your life increasingly sucks.

That is why regularly learning how to diffuse the triggers in yourself is important work. You simply can't feel good or live great until you do. Even if you have material wealth, or are busy indulging yourself in "feel good" activities (food, sex, cigarettes, alcohol, drugs, shopping, thrill seeking adventures), underneath these outer displays triggers (or bombs) lurk.

If you are conscious of these triggers living within you, chances are you will find yourself in a state of chronic anxiety. If you are not conscious of this others may experience themselves as anxious around you. It is as if they are always walking on eggshells. Now you are happy, now you are mad. Now you are easy to be around, now you are an emotional wreck. Others never know what to expect because they never know when they will step on a mine and a bomb will explode in their face.

The only solution is to become your own "bomb squad" and find ways to locate and safely diffuse the various emotional triggers residing within you. That can be done with the help of a trained counselor, or on your own if you are able to consistently use the methods in this book, and some of the techniques that follow.

Diffusing Strong Emotions in Yourself

Knowing more about how to maintain the attitude of the witness, you are more prepared to successfully diffuse strong emotional reactions in yourself, especially when you drop from handling feelings in a healthy way, and start to emote them at the unhealthy levels. This exercise is especially useful when you find yourself caught up in a strong emotional response and need help calming down and refocusing. It is in the nature of a visualization, though it need not be done in a formal manner except when you are dress rehearsing it.

1. If possible as soon as you notice you are triggering off give yourself a "time out." Remove yourself to a quiet space where you can continue to calm down and mentally assess what triggered the emotion in you.

Dr. Lisa Love

2. Then tell yourself to attempt to maintain a calm countenance even though you may be feeling otherwise.
3. Next take a few deep breaths. On the inbreath, use the words "Be my Self," "Renew. On the outbreath, use the words "Let go," "Relax."
4. As you calm down visualize a stream of calming light surrounding and filling you. Know this light to be filled with love and wisdom.
5. Move on and remind yourself that you are the witness (Spirit or soul). Go through a rapid use of the disidentification exercise just given to you. Get into the space of the observer.
6. As you call upon the witness take time to calmly observe the situation that just took place. Then take more time to determine how you could have behaved differently in the situation especially by using the teachings and techniques given later on in this book regarding handling specific feeling states well.
7. Next forgive yourself for having reacted in a strong emotional way, while at the same time resolving to learn from the experience so you can act more skillfully the next time it occurs.
8. As a dress rehearsal remember strong emotional reactions from your past. Consider the circumstances around you which ignited them. Go through the above steps and with each emotional reaction imagine as if this reaction were taking place now. Work with the above until you can see yourself reacting in a more

healthy way. Repeat it this as often as you need to with various situations that trigger you off.

Diffusing Strong Emotions in Others

At times you may be responding in a calm and healthy way emotionally, but others around you may not be. Ideally, whenever you are faced with such a situation, it is best to politely tell the person (on the phone or in person), that you are not able to listen to them in a calm and compassionate way right now, and that you want to "time yourself out" to center yourself and get back to them.

The reason for the language above (saying you will time *yourself* out) is that it avoids a further emotional explosion on the part of the person you are with. First, it is true you are no longer able to handle the person's emotional reaction calmly and compassionately. Second, because this is the case, you need to get away from the individual for your well being, as well as theirs. Third, timing yourself out really times the other person out, giving them space to hopefully calm down. However, there will be occasions when it may not be appropriate to walk away from the individual (such as when an employee is in front of a reactive boss). If so, then this exercise will help you.

1. While with a person who is emotionally reactive lift your point of attention up to the region of your head, approximately three inches in front of your forehead. This helps you call in the witness and acts as a

reminder to be objective and detached in the situation, despite the personal impact it may have on you.
2. If need be, make use of body language and temporarily cross your arms protecting your stomach region. This puts you in touch with your own truth in the situation, and gives you a temporary measure of protection from taking in the blast of emotion.
3. Watch your breathing. Be sure to take slow and steady deep breaths filling up your diaphragm. Attempt to breath from your diaphragm all the way up through your chest, neck, and head. This helps you stay relaxed and get increasingly clear about how to respond to the person.
4. Now, quietly assess the situation. Get curious. You might even ask a few questions silently to yourself such as, why is the person in front of you carrying this emotional intensity? Why is it being released at this moment in time? What is the trigger for this emotional release? What is the person really saying and needing underneath the anger, pain, or fear?
5. Continue to breathe deeply. Send compassion to yourself for having to stay within this difficult situation. And, attempt to let their words pass by you until you are in a compassionate space to listen.
6. When you are ready, respond. You may chose to do this in a number of ways. You can simply assert a powerful statement which says simply, "Enough already. I hear your needs but this is no way to assert them. I am willing to listen to you, and attempt to

meet your needs, but not like this, not until you calm down." Or, you can attempt a compassionate approach, such as gently saying, "You are really upset (or hurt, or afraid) aren't you? Did you have a bad day? Did you need someone to talk to?"

7. As an additional feature, you can also visualize the other person immersed in a blue/white light (which is known to have calming and clarifying effects). However, this technique is only easily done once you have calmed yourself down and have become a compassionate observer. Often this means surrounding yourself in blue/white light first to protect yourself and send compassionate energy to yourself. Then you will be in a better space to attempt to calm down someone else or be compassionate in a calm and reflective way with another.

Part Two

The Major Feeling States

Feeling Good & Living Great

So far in this book you have been given the following tools that fit into a master plan for working with feelings states well so you can feel good and live great.

Initial Stages of the Master Plan

1. As much as possible learn to handle your feeling states as the witness, or observer.
2. Regularly learn to disidentify so that you understand who you really are as the witness, and how you have thoughts, feelings, or actions, but you are not your thoughts, feelings, or actions.
3. Become a mentally polarized individual. This is best done by remembering that your true identity is one of a spiritual being. As that spiritual being spend time cultivating the four levels of mind learning to utilize each in a healthy way.
4. Anchored in the above begin to handle your feeling states at the level of sensation before they become feelings and emotions.
5. If you are unable to do they will shift to the level of feeling. There do your best to work with them at the healthy level or at least within the average range.
6. If you are unable to master your feelings at the healthy level and they slip into emotional reactions then do your best to diffuse your own emotional reactions by following the steps outlined on page 72.
7. Also, make a commitment to get good at going through the initial stages of the master plan so that you

will be less likely to sink into emotionally reactive states.

As indicated there will be times you will not be able to handle your feelings in the most ideal way. That is perfectly ok. Remember for years you have been cultivating certain habit patterns in the way you have handled your feelings and emotions. More than likely it will take time to train yourself in new ways of responding, as well as take time to identify and diffuse emotional triggers. Knowing this be patient with yourself.

The Six Major Feeling States

Once again an important premise of this book is that there are no good or bad feelings. All feelings have a gift to give you and all feelings are your friends. The secret is to shift every feeling from its lower unhealthy state to its higher healthy state so that you can get the gift and learn the lessons that each feeling is attempting to reveal to you. Here then are the six major feelings states and the primary gifts you get out of each when you shift them.

1. Shifting Fear into Love
2. Shifting Confusion into Clarity
3. Shifting Sorrow into Compassion
4. Shifting Anger into Energy
5. Shifting Jealousy into Fulfillment
6. Shifting Happiness into Joy

Feeling Good & Living Great

The following chapters will reveal how to make these shifts by revealing:

1. The gifts and costs of each feeling state if handled or not handled well.
2. The nine levels of each feeling state as they move from healthy, average, to unhealthy levels.
3. The major methods to help you shift each feeling state from its lower to its higher levels of functioning.
4. Additional tips to help you work with each feeling state effectively.
5. Affirmations to assist you in creating constructive thought patterns in regards to each feeling state so you can rapidly default to these healthy thoughts when you start to experience that particular feeling.
6. Visualizations to help you diffuse and remove heavy emotional triggers and patterns.
7. Bach flower remedies that work with each feeling on an energetic level helping you to shift them to higher levels.

Aware of the initial steps of the master plan and the general learnings you will receive regarding each of the six major feeling states, let's go through these feeling states now in more detail.

Shifting Fear Into Love

Feeling Good & Living Great

Fear is an amazing educator. People only fear what they do not understand or don't know how to love. Examine fear more closely and you will see that you are never afraid of people or situations you know and trust.

Fear is overcome through knowledge
and deepening your capacity to love.

Gifts & Costs Of Fear

Why knowledge? Because once you have an intelligent understanding of how to effectively work with any situation your fear will lesson or go away all together. Why love? Because love allows you to both face and embrace something. And, as you learn to love what you fear it becomes impossible to be afraid any longer.

I am reminded of a time in my twenties when I enjoyed rock climbing. One day as my partner and I were preparing our ropes to start a climb, a young man next to us began his ascent using no ropes or safety devices whatsoever. For some time I watched as this man made his way past numerous climbers. Eventually, he reached a difficult section that two climbers were attempting to navigate around for some time. To my amazement the young man nimbly went around them and even appeared to leap in the air to get clear of them as he continued.

It occurred to me that this young man was either courageous, crazy, or both. How could he do such a thing with so little fear or hesitation? Obviously, he was a very skilled climber who apparently had a great deal of knowledge regarding this particular rock face. He may have even climbed it hundreds of times already possibly using ropes when he first learned how to do so. Knowledge had helped him overcome fear, but why risk his life by not using safety devices while doing so? Clearly he had reached a point where he loved rock climbing more than he loved life itself. He may have even arrived at that place where his love of climbing without ropes had overcome his fear of death. Thus, he could tell himself if he was going to die it might as well happen doing something he totally loved.

How can you get to a place where whenever you feel fear you can derive it's gifts and avoid it's cost? To begin with whenever you are confronted with fear ask the following questions.

In what areas do I need to increase my knowledge so I can cope with and eliminate my fear effectively?

How can I learn to love what I fear so I can move it into a positive direction?

Fear then is a wake up call asking you to become more aware and alert regarding what is happening around you. And, where possible fear is attempting to show you how you can become more understanding and loving in relation to who or whatever you fear. Cultivating greater knowledge and love in regards to what you fear takes time. When you do not have that knowledge or love it is best to move away from who or what is triggering your fear. Still it is good to consider the costs of not shifting your fear as you make that decision to move away. Costs include:

1. A dulled sensitivity to what is going on within and without preventing you from perceiving threats.
2. An inability to access your intuition so you can discover innovative solutions and fresh ideas that can help you solve challenges you face.
3. A freezing of your overall awareness, mental clarity, and emotional poise making you believe you have no way to cope with what you are afraid of.
4. A failure to take healthy risks and to live a meaningful life that is so full of love you are even able to face the ultimate fear — death — with courage and grace.

Levels Of Fear

Healthy Fear Zone — Lesson: Pay Attention

1. Tense — Become alert to what is around you.
2. Troubled — Learn what you need to pay attention to.
3. Timid — Discover if you can handle it well.

Average Fear Zone — Lesson: Get Competent & Love

4. Worried — Keep a reasonable state of mind.
5. Anxious — Breathe to stabilize yourself.

6. Fearful — Stay poised and get more educated.

Unhealthy Fear Zone — Lesson: Avoid the Shut Down

7. Panicky — Stay calm even if making an exit.
8. Terrified — Call on knowledge and love to cope.
9. Horrified — Avoid freezing or threat will get you.

As you work with fear you will only be able to do so if you can maintain the attitude of the witness or observer and stay open to all four levels of your mind. Then you will stay in the healthy fear zone where fear will be handled more at the level of sensation with its gifts given to you more rapidly, and where you will work with fear more effectively. Otherwise, you will drop to the average zone where fear is now colored with greater feeling tones. Here fear can still be managed, but if it is not handled well it will start to elicit more of an emotional response as your capacity to maintain the attitude of the witness is dropped. Once you are in the unhealthy zone, your fear will become much more emotionally charged, reactive, and triggered. Now your fear will be very difficult to manage and may leave emotional scars that will need to be healed later. Let's examine those three zones now.

As revealed above fear shows up first in the healthy zone as a tendency to be tense, troubled, and timid because there is something you are not paying attention to and need to. For example, maybe you are getting a signal that your job may be insecure. By deciding to pay attention right away you can begin to glean knowledge. Is there something you need to do to up your performance level? Do you need to build stronger communications with those around you? Is there somewhere you need to implement more love? Do you truly love and enjoy what you do? If you don't can you find a way to love it more, or do you need to move on? By asking questions like these you activate your intuitive and logical minds soon enough to help you learn from your fear quickly so you can handle what is coming up in a more effective way.

Miss these opportunities and you are likely to slip into the average fear zone where you succumb to the delusion that you have no way to cope effectively because you can no longer intuit or logically discern where effective coping solutions may be found. Now you may start to worry, then become increasingly anxious, until finally you get fearful. Sadly, all these feeling states tend to dull your ability to calmly witness and observe. They also prevent you from acting quickly and effectively.

As you slip into worry for example you may start to create excessive mental chatter where your thoughts obsess on the problem without successfully helping you find solutions. Instead of being able to gain real knowledge, your mind may spin and loop over and over again on the same issue. For example you might say to yourself, "Am I going to lose my job? Have people stopped liking me? Does my boss think I am no longer good at what I do?" The problem with these questions is that they are not solution oriented because they focus more on yes and no answers than on genuine intuitive and logical or objective inquiry.

Since solutions are not arising you now become anxious where you begin to feel that you can't cope with what is happening. Fear is the natural next step as your mind makes increasingly irrational and exaggerated statements like, "Oh my, I don't think I can deal with this. This is so awful." Or, "I've faced something like this before and failed, I know I will only fail again." These kinds of thoughts only increase the fear, agitation, and anxiety making it likely that you will react in ways that don't serve you.

Refuse to handle your fears in an effective way from this point forward and you may now enter the unhealthy levels of fear. Here you panic and fail to act skillfully, numb out, or fail to react at all. So, you just sit there frozen by your fear. Living like an automaton, others now have the capacity to use your fear to take advantage of you. They may even attempt to keep you in a state of fear so they can get power over you causing you to surrender your money, freedom, and even your soul.

Once at this level it is imperative that you deal with what is happening immediately through an act of courageous will. From there you must re-engage all four levels of your mind, hook up to your spiritual self, calm yourself down emotionally, and summon your courage so you can deal with what is going on. If you don't the threat will overcome you causing you serious damage and in some cases even death in the process.

Feeling Good & Living Great

Both the unhealthy and average levels of fear can be avoided if you remember there is such a thing as healthy fear that encourages you to get rapid insight so you can take healthy risks. Healthy risks come about from engaging the witness and using your intuitive and logical minds to increase the probability of risks working out in your favor. Healthy risks also engage the motivational and instinctual minds in the right way so that you act with skill and right timing. Plus, when you add love to the equation healthy fear gives you the courage to act in a positive way, since courage and love often go together.

Also, healthy risks are a part of healthy action. Risks encourage you to try out new things in life. They help you to grow and flex your muscles — spiritual, mental, emotional, and physical. Engaged in exploring and mastering new things risk helps you feel alive and make life more worth living. It is often said that people who have great success in life are those who have taken great risks even if it meant they sometimes resulted in failure. Since every failure was turned into an opportunity to learn and to love even failures encouraged those taking healthy risks to take some more without being afraid of doing so.

Lose your ability to learn from fear and take healthy risks and you may not only lose out on your capacity to enjoy life, you may even lose some of your dignity and self-worth because you end up feeling like a fool. You only end up being a fool in the true sense, however, when you are not using fear to your advantage so it increases your capacity to learn and love. Fail to learn and you will end up looking like a fool causing your sense of self-worth and self-love to diminish. Then you may never want to take risks of any kind and fear will have won out leaving you full of emotional triggers and pain.

Main Methods for Shifting Fear

If fear does start to take you over then in addition to the initial stages of the master plan these major techniques will help.

Deep Breathing. One of the best ways to start managing fear is through the practice of deep belly breathing. Fear often causes you to breath in a shallow and quick way from the level of your upper chest. Shallow chest breathing also causes your nervous system to become hyper-sensitive, speeds up your heart-rate, and blocks the flow of oxygen to your brain shutting down your higher reasoning processes.

Deep belly breathing has the reverse effect. It sharpens your senses, calms your heart rate, and provides extra oxygen to your brain intensifying your ability to think intuitively and rationally. Martial artists are keenly aware of this, which is one reason they learn to move the breath and the body as a unit allowing them to enhance their perceptions. For example, as a fist or kick moves towards them it might appear to do so in slow motion giving them the ability to observe the way in which the attack is approaching them so they can rapidly deflect it.

Likewise, as you breathe deeply things may appear

to slow down giving you the capacity to assess what is going on more clearly. The end result is right action allowing you to send away what you don't want so you can better attract what you do want once this fearful element is no longer hindering you.

Desensitization. Desensitization is a fancy word for learning how to become less sensitive or fearful. To desensitize you need to slowly acclimate to whatever is making you afraid by learning to be around it in gradual and small ways. This slow process helps you challenge various instinctual mind reactions that trigger a state of hyper-arousal and teaches your instinctual mind instead to be less reactive and more calm.

As this happens you are able to access your intuition and logic giving you the knowledge you need to manage your fear in the best way. Plus, you can reprogram your fear through affirmations that engage your motivational mind and enhance your ability to trust that you can move beyond fear into faith. All of this keeps you from being overly sensitive and allows you to manage your fear so it no longer interferes in your life.

Reduce Stimulation. As mentioned fear by necessity starts the process of activating a state of hyper-arousal that either helps or hinders you. An example of helpful hyper-arousal includes swerving out of the way when a car suddenly moves into your lane on the freeway nearly causing an accident. An example of it hindering you is when you veer out of the way to miss the car coming at you, but move too far in the other direction hitting another car yourself.

The tendency to over-react often means that you are living too much in a state of constant hyper-arousal. Removing or reducing stimulants out of your life is one way to counter this. Caffeinated drinks or products, loud sounds and music, bright lights, events or situations that bring about a fearful state (including the consumption of movies and TV shows that induce fear), are all best avoided until your hyper state of arousal is gone. In place of these over-stimulating activities try cultivating methods that help you relax such as using drinks and products that calm you, surrounding yourself with quiet sounds and peaceful music, engaging in relaxation and meditation practices, spending time in tranquil spaces and more!

<u>Unify With Your Fear</u>. A favorite lesson of mine for how to work with fear comes from the book, *Dune*. A futuristic story *Dune* is famous for its saying about how to handle fear. It goes as follows, "I must not fear. Fear is the mind killer. Fear is the little-death that brings total obliteration. I will face my fear. I will permit it to pass over me and through me. And when it has gone past I will turn the inner eye to see its path. Where the fear has gone there will be nothing. Only I will remain."

As the saying reveals, fear really *is* the mind killer and it *does* bring about death at many levels. But, as you face fear and let it pass over and through you, your senses wake up allowing you to become intensely alert. From that space you can attract the courage you need to defeat the fear inside and outside of you. You open up to the inner eye, which is the "eye of Spirit" reflecting down into your mind to activate your intuition giving you the ideas and insight you need regarding how best to cope.

Then your fear dissolves and turns into a dance where the unknown elements that are creating your fear reveal themselves and move into a more harmonious state. As they become increasingly known to each other and understood they further enter into a state of love and become a single unified "I" working harmoniously together.

As fear is countered with love you learn to become more sensitive, knowledgeable, and empathetic with whatever or whomever you fear. Instead of opposing them you are inclined to ask questions, engage in dialogue, expand your understanding, and open your heart some more. In this way you dissolve the blocks to love in regards to what you fear and come to understand it better through the power of love.

Cultivate Courage. A few years ago I was asked to write a series of unique movie reviews for a company I helped to found called *LoveMovies!* These movie reviews focused on lessons from films that either celebrated the presence of love or revealed the lack of it in various films. At the time the *Harry Potter* movies were hugely successful so I did a review and decided the main lesson from the overall series of movies was "Dare to Love." That's because I felt Harry was constantly overcoming adverse and terrifying situations through love and courage.

Courage is a word that essentially means "take heart." When you have courage you are asked to move into your heart and reminded to ask yourself the question of who and what you love enough to motivate you into service and loving action. As you do so even if great sacrifices may be involved (including that of your own life), you move forward so you can change your life and the lives of those around you for the better.

Because of Harry's love for his friends he was likewise compelled into numerous acts of courage. And, it may be that only love compels any of us to face our fears to such an extent that we put our lives at risk. So, when you or someone you love is afraid, you can ask them, "Who or what do you love enough to keep on going?" That's how Harry overcomes his fears. He constantly remembers those he loves and finds a way to feel their love in return so he can conquer his fears by doing so. And, that is how you can learn to overcome many of your fears as well. (Note: To access this and other movie reviews or to obtain free gifts visit my website at www.doctorlisalove.com).

More Tips For Overcoming Fear

1. *Educate yourself.* Once you know what you are dealing with you won't feel so afraid anymore.
2. *Turn your anxiety into action.* Get busy doing something about your problems. Remember it is better to try something than nothing at all.
3. *Vocalize.* It's no accident that people often yell in the face of fear. Sound your battle cry (whatever that is)

and then boldly move forward.
4. *Rake it till you make it*. Pretend you are not afraid and you may discover you might not be.
5. *Rally the troops*. Remember sometimes there is strength in numbers so enlist others for support.
6. *Stay in the stream of love*. Spend as much time as you can being surrounded by loving people, reading and listening to loving conversations, keeping open to love in it's many forms, and praying to become a more loving person. Remember love overcomes fear, births courage, and ultimately gives you what you need to really feel good and live great in life.

Fear Affirmations

Following are some great affirmations to help you better manage your fears.

1. Here and now I cultivate greater calm, clarity, and insight to help me manage my fears more effectively.
2. More and more I intuit what I need to help me handle my fears well.
3. Each and every day I create safety zones by attracting to myself people who support and protect me, safe places to live, and the knowledge of how I can better build and live within a safe world.
4. I love knowing that I can learn to manage areas that cause me fear so that I experience greater protection and peace of mind in my life.

Dr. Lisa Love

Fear Visualization

Releasing the Basket. Begin by assuming a comfortable position either sitting or lying down. Make sure you are physically relaxed, but not to a point of total relaxation.Now, close your eyes and try to imagine yourself in a field of green grass. Use all your senses to help you make this place seem real to you. Look in all directions and identify visually as much as you can. Get in touch with the colors around you. Experience the touch of the grass under your feet, gentle breezes brushing your skin, the warmth of the sun on your face, arms, legs, and torso. Listen for any sounds such as birds singing, trees rustling, or animals scrambling. Realize any smells that may be coming from the flowers or trees.

Now, imagine a balloon anchored to the ground near you. Pay attention to its colors, size, texture, smell, dimension, etc. Notice that the balloon is anchored by a number of stakes that keep it from flying away. See also that the basket is empty. As you look inside the basket let your mind move naturally to something you greatly desire. Maybe it is financial security, a love relationship, greater health, and so on. Once you have identified what you want imagine that you are placing that want into the basket. You can either see it written down on a piece of paper that you put in the basket or see it as a symbol.

After you have put your want into the basket, imagine as if your fears are anchoring you to the Earth like stakes in the ground. Understand that you will not get what you want until you have released your "stake" in not having your wants met. Go from stake to stake and identify the fear attached to each one. Maybe a stake represents a fear that you will have less freedom if you get the job you want. Or, a stake could stand for feeling rejected again if you attempt to attract a person you can love into your life.

After each fear is formulated clearly in your mind shift your focus to counter your fears by increasing your desire to have what you want over what you don't want. If need be see your desire to be free from what you fear fueling the balloon above the basket with air, so much so the basket is capable of breaking the rope that keeps it held to the stakes on the ground. (Important, leave the stakes behind. Do not bring your fears with you as the basket breaks free). Then, as the balloon and basket break free notice how good it feels to finally be able to release your fears below.

Next, as you watch the basket and the balloon moving upward see them catapult toward the sun overhead. Know that the sun is activating your intuition to give you fresh ideas for coping, as well as your logic to give you the practical steps you need to help you turn your desires into a reality. As you put your focus more on the sun and less on the basket, allow your intuition to create a symbol that will convey a message of how you can have what you want (and what Spirit wants for you) in a more wise and courageous way.

As the symbol emerges notice how the heat of the

sun suddenly pops the balloon and disintegrates the basket. As all of this happens let your intuitive mind be filled with light and let insights come to you regarding what you need to do right now to make your dreams become a reality at this point in your life. Then take time to consider, "How does it feel to have this insight in your hands? How does it feel to know that you can have what you want, and what Spirit wants for you?"

Close the exercise by using the wisdom and insight you gained to help you formulate a resolution to make any necessary changes you need to in your life so you can finally be free of your fear. Allow your fear to be replaced by love and notice how much better your life is because of this. Take as much time as you need to experience this. Then, when you are ready, gently open your eyes, and conclude by writing down everything you remember about this experience. (Note: These visualizations are available to you on a CD by Dr. Lisa Love. Visit her website at www.doctorlisalove.com to learn more).

Fear Bach Flowers

Bach Flowers are flower essences that you take in small dozes over a long period of time that are said to have healing effects primarily on your emotions. For the skeptical homeopathic remedies like the Bach Flowers may seem like a waste of time. But, having actively used them for years, I believe they work. And, they only cost about ten dollars a vial, which typically lasts for months.

Feeling Good & Living Great

Here are the ones for fear:

- Apprehension & Anxiety: Aspen
- Afraid to Say No: Century
- Doubting Self: Cerato
- Fear of Losing Control: Cherry Plum
- Fear of Losing Someone You Love: Chicory
- Fear of Failure: Larch
- Fear of Everyday Situations: Mimulus
- Anxiety That Those You Love Will Be Harmed: Red Chestnut
- Terror & Panic: Rock Rose
- Fear of Not Being Perfect: Rock Water

Shifting Confusion Into Clarity

Feeling Good & Living Great

Of all the emotions confusion is perhaps the most benign on the surface. Yet, though it is not as intense in its emotional display as other emotional expressions may be, confusion can create numerous difficulties in your life, especially when it freezes you up, hinders your ability to act, and stops you from living at the level of your soul so you can attract what is truly best for you in your life. Whenever confusion enters your life, understand it carries the following message:

Confusion is asking you to get humble and seek clarity regarding the best direction to go.

Gifts & Costs of Confusion

To counter confusion with clarity you need to know how to tap into Spirit so you can hook up to your intuitive mind where fresh insights into how to resolve your life difficulties can occur. As these "ah-ha" moments are received you can then activate the logical part of your mind to help you sort out what the practical steps are that you need to take to get to where you need to go. If you are having trouble tapping into both your intuition and your logic ask yourself the following:

How do I need to surrender and let Spirit guide me through this process?

Dr. Lisa Love

How can I relax and live more in the moment so I can better open up to what Spirit is wanting from me?

Confusion is in many ways a signal for a time out so that you can call upon Spirit and the witness to help you reflect and get perspective. Often confusion happens because you are no longer heading in a direction that is in alignment with where Spirit wants you to go. That is why instead of mucking around in a state of confusion it is best to take the time to realign by calling in the witness and allowing the "fog lights" of Spirit and your intuitive mind to help lead you in the direction you need to go. If you don't then you may be subjected to the costs of confusion that include the following:

1. Paralysis caused by over-analysis as the logical mind over complicates things and blocks the intuitive mind from offering positive solutions.
2. Fence sitting behaviors that prevent you from making choices and accepting responsibility for them.
3. Negative health impacts especially from headaches that can emerge when you try too hard from an ego level to get the solution you want, instead of opening up to the solution that is attempting to find you.
4. Turning your decision making process too frequently over to others who may not make the best decisions on your behalf, or who resent how weak you have become because you fail to decide for yourself.

5. Staying stuck in irrational beliefs that keep you from breaking through confusion because you think there is one perfect answer and you can't do anything until you find it, or you believe there is no answer at all.

Levels Of Confusion

Healthy Confusion Zone — Lesson: Cultivate Humility

1. Ambivalent — Admit something is there to look at.
2. Uneasy — Be humble & realize you need clarity.
3. Unclear — Get quiet and then sort out what to do.

Average Confusion Zone — Lesson: Stay Open

4. Confused — Admit you don't know correct choice.
5. Overwhelmed — Start to remove too many options.
6. Worried — Focus on solution instead of problem.

Unhealthy Confusion Zone — Lesson: Don't Lose Hope

7. Perplexed — Decide to act even if you make a mistake.
8. Lost — Stand still and let intuition/logic guide you.
9. Paralyzed — Keep it simple, go one step at a time.

Especially when you are attempting to come from your soul instead of your ego you need to surrender and open up to what Spirit is trying reveal to you regarding the present situation you are in. In fact, confusion can be a sign of spiritual growth because it forces you to let go of your ego that typically wants you to believe that you have all the answers. When these answers don't work and confusion sets in it is time to be humble enough to admit that there is something you don't know. That's why confusion can often be a signal from Spirit trying to tell you that you need to attract something new into your life apart from what you are stubbornly hanging onto.

    A classic film I like along these lines is the movie *Cast Away* starring actor Tom Hanks. At the start of this film Tom's character, Chuck Noland, is overly preoccupied with his work. He also has a nasty habit of attempting to control everything in his life by always filling up his time with to-do's and deadlines. Then, while flying overseas his plane crashes in the ocean and he becomes the sole survivor on a desert island. Lost and dazed, Chuck first has to overcome his overwhelm and disbelief regarding what has happened. Once he does so he draws upon his instinctual mind (what he already knows) and creates a signal so others can see he needs help.

    When this does not work, he uses his motivational and logical minds to build a raft to leave the island. Sadly, the materials at hand are not enough to help him build a sufficient raft to leave. Slowly, he surrenders and adapts to his fate remaining in a confused state about how to finally get home. Then, one day, a piece of plane wreckage washes ashore giving him the means to get out of there. Once home, Chuck retains the valuable lessons he has learned on the island, including living life in a more flexible way and worrying less about being in control.

Confusion is very much like this. It throws you into an unknown realm where you are often brought to your knees in humility staring up at Spirit like a helpless child looking for signs that will help you know which way to go. Confusion throws your ego into turmoil, revealing ways you have become over-confident and rigid in your beliefs as to how your life should turn out. But, with humility you can move forward and intuit answers of where to go. And, humility is an important ingredient as we move through the healthy, average, and unhealthy zones.

To deal with confusion effectively then your ego must admit that there is something it doesn't know. Only in this way will you stay in the healthy confusion zone. Of course not knowing requires an act of surrender allowing you to access your intuitive mind and discover the solutions you need too. Blatantly refusing to surrender usually means your ego believes it knows everything and takes on a "been there, done that," "yeah, but" or "nothing will work" attitude. Of course if you believe there is nothing you can learn then in fact there is nothing you will learn, because you have already closed off access to your intuitive mind where solutions exist for you.

Unfortunately, the longer you refuse to be humble and surrender, the more you will descend into the average confusion zone where confusion starts to overwhelm you. Here you may also worry about not making a decision or making the wrong decision. For this reason you may fail to decide or act at all. Now you avoid taking responsibility for your life since you don't want to be blamed for making mistakes or failing in any way. But, allowing yourself to make mistakes and taking responsibility for learning from them is part of maturing as a human being.

Also, when you live too much in a state of worry you get other people frustrated with you as you refuse to make a decision, wanting them to do it for you. That is why it is better for you to wake up, become conscious, and move beyond ignorance and confusion into the realm where you can make positive and dynamic choices that allow you to lead a more fulfilling life.

When you refuse to do this your confusion descends even further into the unhealthy levels. Here you may not only become perplexed, you can be set adrift making you feel lost. The more lost you feel the more doubt will descend upon you moving you into a place of inaction and resignation. Here you can end up feeling completely frozen and paralyzed. Trapped in this space you have no choice but to do something, even if it is only taking one simple step at a time in a particular direction.

Main Methods for Shifting Confusion

Rest. Often people in a state of confusion are really just too tired to think. That is why it is essential whenever you feel confusion to be sure you get plenty of rest. Rest helps you better access your intuitive mind so you can gain inspiration regarding which direction to go. Rest helps you feel more relaxed and patient, increasing the odds you will make the best decision according to your best knowledge and intent. Rest keeps your overall emotional vibration attuned to a lighter and more optimistic state. And, it prevents you from trying too hard, or losing momentum before you have tried hard enough.

You can also help yourself get enough rest by avoiding too much stimulation. On a mental level that stimulation tends to come about through over-analysis, which as the saying goes can lead you to paralysis. On a physical level, you can induce greater states of rest if you avoid too much stimulant intake such as coffee, tea, herbal energy boosters, diet pills and other activities that might make you overly hyper and alert.

Learn from the Past. In a classic scene from the film *The Lion King*, Simba the lion, is contemplating taking his father's place to become king. Talking to his advisor Rafiki, Simba reveals that he is hesitant to become king primarily because he believes he will have to confront the pain he experienced when he witnessed his father's murder. Rather than face his past he wants to ignore it and just move on with his life. In response to this Rafiki hits Simba on the head with his stick. Simba crys out and says, "Ow! Jeez, what was that for?" Rafiki replies, "It doesn't matter. It's in the past." Simba rubs his head and says, "Yeah, but it still hurts." "Oh yes, the past can hurt," Rafiki shares, "But the way I see it, you can either run from it, or learn from it." Having said this Rafiki swings his stick again, but this time, having learned his lesson Simba ducks out of the way.

Though the past can hold you back if you dwell on it too long, taking time to integrate the lessons of your past can help you avoid making the same mistakes over and over again. After all, confusion often happens because you are thinking, feeling, and acting in worn out ways that don't allow you to get the results you want. Only by taking time to see how your previous mistakes have hindered you, can you discover how to stop repeating these mistakes and move forward in a more constructive way. Then your confidence and your ability to make course corrections will increase allowing you to move one step further towards your achieving your goals.

Live in the Now. Living in the present moment is another vital process for helping you breakthrough confusion. When you fully live in the present moment you are able to open up to the beauty and joy that still exists all around you. And, it helps you stay open to your intuitive mind where guidance and fresh insights can come to you. The present moment also has the power to heighten your senses allowing you to experience greater clarity and illuminate your life.

But, there is a big difference between living in the now in a way that helps you pay attention to what you need to in the moment, and living in the moment in a way that causes you to avoid your responsibilities and lessons through escapist and addictive behaviors. That is why it is good to understand that the true "now" isn't just knowing how to experience this second in the realm of time. It is knowing how to live more fully within the *larger spec-*

trum of time. Then, you get insights into what priorities and values you need to be attending to in this moment so that the past/present/future (that comprise the Eternal Now) are all lived along more spiritual lines. Living in this kind of "now" brings tremendous clarity and expands your world view. And, it gives you the power to include more in any present moment because that moment is filled not with just hedonistic indulgences to your senses, but with greater insight, wisdom, peace, clarity, and calm.

<u>Risk</u>. Sometimes when you are confused it is better to try something than nothing at all. Ideally, this something is based upon a calculated risk that engages your logical mind not just your instinctual mind, increasing your odds for success. Still, at some point you have to stop thinking or talking about it, and just do something to get you moving and acting in a certain direction, whether you know what you are doing or not.

Failing to act is usually based upon fear and not just confusion. Maybe you are afraid to make a mistake, maybe because you have made so many already you don't want to make the same mistake over and over again. But, at some point you have to take a risk and do something. If you are afraid of the outcome think of it this way, it won't be as bad as you think. Because chances are you have learned at least something from your mistakes in the past. And, even if you fail again most likely you will still be one step closer to where you really want to be because you know one more route not to take. So, yes, take some time to think things through then stop procrastinating and do something, because next time it may really work out.

Consciously Complain. A new trend in recent years is summarized in the popular phrase, "No whining." The idea behind this notion is that anytime you complain about something it is totally unproductive and a bad thing. True, when you complain about something as a means to just sit on the fence and spin your wheels, it is not productive. I remember a client of mine who was very good at this. He was attempting to decide whether he should stay with his girlfriend or leave her. We discussed both options together, but instead of acting on either he would call and just want to complain about it. It reminded me of a saying, "Deciding not to decide is deciding."

But, there is another form of complaining that isn't about sitting there and doing nothing. Known as conscious complaining, this process helps you sort out what is going on in a situation confronting you. As you sort it out you may get clearer about what you do and do not want regarding whatever is confronting you. Sifting back and forth you may even finally come up with a solution that feels good and can lead to living great if you act upon it.

More Tips For Overcoming Confusion

1. *Be still and know*. Though it is tempting to approach confusion mainly at the level of gaining knowledge, confusion is ultimately diminished when you become silent and access the intuitional levels of you mind touching your soul.

2. <u>Tackle one small thing at a time</u> to eliminate overwhelm. Avoid focusing too much on the big picture or you may feel it is impossible to succeed. Rather focus on what is right in front of you so you can turn mountains into molehills, and then nothing at all.
3. <u>Avoid mental fatigue by helping your mind calm down</u>. Meditate. Distract it with other activities. Engage in play. Take a nap. Go for a walk. Do yoga and breath work. Watch or do something silly. Remember sometimes it helps to let go and let Spirit do the work!

Confusion Affirmations

1. Here and now I release my attachment to how things should resolve themselves so I can stay clear and open regarding how things are meant to work out.
2. More and more I use rest, meditation, and prayer to assist me in overcoming confusion and to bring greater clarity and calm into my life.
3. Each and every day I prioritize, organize, and learn to delegate what I need to so I reduce the odds of confusion and free myself up to master what I need to.
4. I love knowing that I can live fully in the moment attending to what I need to so I can benefit more fully.

Confusion Visualization

<u>Radiant Sun</u>. As with any visualization begin by sitting in a comfortable chair with your spine erect and

feet on the floor (or with your legs supported underneath you in a comfortable cross-legged position). Gently close your eyes and allow your attention to focus on your breathing, simply watching the natural rhythm of your breath rise and fall.

Next, move your attention to your physical body allowing it to gradually relax. Notice if you are hunching your shoulders and if you are let them relax more freely on each side. Be sure that you are not holding tension in your stomach and if need be let it simply hang out without letting a belt or tension constrict it. If your neck is tight, gently roll it from side to side and front to back. Relax your arms and legs more fully if need be. Then pay additional attention to the muscles in your face being sure to keep your jaw relaxed, your forehead and cheek muscles relaxed, the tiny muscles around the eyes relaxed, and even consider relaxing the back of your tongue so it rests comfortably in your mouth.

Take a few deep breaths and then turn your attention to your feelings. Visualize them coming to rest seeing them become calm and serene like a still pool of crystal clear blue water. Continue to breathe slowly and naturally in and out allowing any ripples of emotional upset to diminish and become tranquil. Just allow yourself to be in a place of emotional peace for now.

Once you feel emotionally calm, take three steady, deep, and diaphragmatic breaths. With each breath lift your focus of attention upwards to a place approximately three inches in front of the physical forehead. This is the region you naturally lift into whenever you are attempting to get insight into any situation. As you lift your attention there use your creative imagination to see a small golden sun forming in this region. As the light of this sun intensifies, imagine this light is being thrown down and outward so that it slowly envelopes your entire physical body gently warming your body as it does so. Let this light seep into every pore of your body gently illumining your brain and nervous system. Remember to keep this a sensorial experience and not a thinking one.

After you experience a warm sensation throughout your body use your imagination to direct the light from this sun to illuminate any particular area you are having difficulty with in your life. Let the light from this sun clarify what you are struggling with. Then, let your thought processes be activated so an insight or two can come into your awareness. Do not force the process.

Continue to stay with the flow of insights for approximately five to ten minutes. If no insights arise stay within the sensation of light and know they will come of their own accord later throughout the next day or two. Upon completion of this exercise, gently open your eyes and write down any insights which may have occurred. Take your time as you come out of the meditation, as some people may feel a little disoriented when doing so.

Confusion Bach Flowers

- Second Guessing Yourself: Cerato

Dr. Lisa Love

- Failure to Learn from Mistakes: Chestnut Bud
- Spacey & Absent Minded: Clematis
- Overwhelmed by Responsibilities: Elm
- Doubting Things Will Improve: Gorse
- Stuck in the Past: Honeysuckle
- Procrastination: Hornbeam
- Afraid to Attempt Anything: Larch
- Burdened by Too Many Responsibilities: Oak
- Difficulty Making Decisions: Scleranthus
- Totally Uncertain: Wild Oat

Shifting Sorrow Into Compassion

Feeling Good & Living Great

No one moves through life without being touched by sorrow. Anytime you experience loss sorrow emerges to help you cope, release, heal, and move on. Sorrow can also include regret, which happens when you feel sorry (or sorrowful) for something you, or someone else, said or did that was harmful. Sorrow may also show you how you could have handled a situation in a more positive and loving way leading you to this realization:

Sorrow opens you up to greater insight, humility and compassion.

Gifts & Costs of Sorrow

Though sorrow can feel difficult the more fully you can let go and empty out regarding any loss, the more space you create in yourself for renewal, rejuvenation, and even joy. The following questions help you do this.

What do I need to let go of at this point in my life before I attract something new?

What lessons do I need to learn that will help me use this loss in a soulful way?

When it comes to letting go you might discover that you are being faced with releasing a loved person, job, or cherished belief. Perhaps you need to let go of the notion of how life should be and accept it more as it is.

Maybe you need to forgive yourself or others regarding mistakes that might have been made in relation to your loss. Or, maybe you need to listen to what might be experienced as a gentle tug at your heart, which is there to remind you about your interconnection with all of life.

Whatever you need to release take time to really feel your loss. I call it wringing out the sponge because sorrow is like having a sponge full of water. The only way to lighten up the sponge is to wring out all the water by feeling and releasing your sorrow at a deep level. If you don't feel your sadness or sorrow fully and attempt to talk yourself out of it in a premature way, you can actually do more harm than good. Why? Because every unresolved level of sadness or sorrow acts like an anchor dragging you backwards no matter how hard you try to move forward resulting in some of the following costs:

1. Disconnection from the sorrows of the world making you increasingly insensitive as a human being.
2. Oversensitivity to the sorrows of the world immobilizing you from doing anything productive.
3. Discounting an opportunity to take responsibility for any thoughts and behaviors that may be contributing to the suffering of yourself or others.
4. Refusing to be more humble as you recognize there are some things you simply cannot control.
5. Not letting sorrow free you from attachments to incompatible people, unhealthy behaviors, and outworn ideas.

Feeling Good & Living Great

Levels Of Sorrow

Healthy Sorrow Zone — Lesson: Cultivate Detachment

1. Missing — Embrace what you miss with love.
2. Disappointed — Let go and stay open to possibilities.
3. Gloomy — Look for the open "possibility" window.

Average Sorrow Zone — Lesson: Get Ready to Release

4. Sad — Empty out and release the old.
5. Sorrowful — Have compassion for your loss.
6. Grieving — Realize what you had will never return.

Unhealthy Sorrow Zone — Lesson: Reattach to Spirit

7. Helpless — Reach out to others to help you cope.
8. Despondent — Get support groups around you.
9. Suicidal — Get immediate professional help.

The anchor effect of sorrow often explains why despite all the happy feelings you may attempt to generate at the level of your motivational mind to get ahead when you start to feel sad it remains difficult. But, you don't remove an anchor by pretending it just isn't there. You remove it by getting rid of it, which you will only do when you learn to keep sorrow mostly in the healthy versus average and unhealthy zones.

Ideally sorrow is released first and foremost at the healthy levels by remembering the love. Do this by remembering how you loved what you lost and how it loved you. As you release what you have loved you can find ways to help that love continue to live into the future in the way of memories, memorials and even foundations that help honor your loved one.

If you cannot release in this way then it is important to look for the silver lining, or the open window, in your loss. Sometimes this is done by finding new possibilities that elicit your love and compassion. For example, maybe there are people around you who are also suffering a loss and would benefit from you being able to share empathy with them. Or, maybe there are new people (pets, places, items) that you will be able to love in the future. Staying open in this way helps you turn your sorrow into compassion and keeps you from sinking into greater levels of disappointment and gloom.

But, if you find it difficult to move forward and manage your sorrow well you will break down into the average levels where the feeling of loss becomes heavier moving you into the stages of sadness, sorrow, and grief. Though you might think you can deny your loss and not do the necessary work of letting go, a failure to do this will only prolong your sorrow. True, loss is loss and in the words of the famous poem by Dusty Bunker called *To Heal Again,* loss "takes as long as it takes." Still, loss doesn't have to cut as deep if you go through the necessary processes of healing to help it along.

If you refuse to let go, however, you might sink into the place where sorrow shifts into helplessness, despair, and even suicidal gestures. Suicide is basically a feeling that you have no way out of the predicament you are in. Once you feel you are out of ideas or solutions to improve your life, helplessness and hopelessness cascade down upon you like an oppressive acid rain. Only an act of total surrender to Spirit, where you admit you simply do not have the answers to your life problems, will help you get free of your current predicament. By letting go of the old so you can radically leap into something new, you can come back to a place of hope and renewal where you can feel free to live in love and joy again.

Finally, as you turn your overall sorrow into compassion it in turn helps you cultivate faith that in time life will bring you renewed opportunities to both love and be loved again. It may even be possible that you will experience even more fulfilling attachments, beliefs, behaviors, ideas, and people in your life than you did before. And, as your sorrow turns into compassion it may even lead you into profound states of peace and calm as you enter into the silence, listen to your soul's wisdom, and surrender your sadness and sorrow in such a way it connects you to humanity as a whole. Expanded into your connection with the entire human family you will be even more likely to become open to new inspirations and possibilities regarding how best to live your life from this point forward.

Dr. Lisa Love

Main Methods for Shifting Sorrow

<u>Cry</u>. Especially when you are confronted with releasing someone or something crying is very useful. Tears even have beneficial biological functions. Tears are said to cleanse your eyes, which on a psychological level is symbolic of helping you to see things clearer. Tears also clean out your sinuses, and sinus problems are said to be related to congestion and irritation due to an inability to let go of the frustration you may be feeling regarding things not going your way. Tears release toxins from the body, which symbolize attachments that have become toxic because they are no longer nourishing you, or are taking you away from where you need to be right now at this stage of your life. And, crying can restore you to a state of deep peace, which is why many people say they feel rejuvenated, refreshed, and ready to move on with life once their tears have finally subsided!

In many ways crying helps you to wring out the sponge of grief. Giving yourself time and space to grieve is essential. Since sorrow is often a shunned emotion, you might need to find a private and peaceful place to get fully in touch with it. Such places are typically beautiful and inspiring in some way. They may consist of a church/temple/mosque, a spot in nature, a room, your bathroom, car, or anywhere where you can feel free to be fully yourself. Whatever place becomes your sacred space for grieving use it to help you enrich your sense of love, compassion, and peace.

Feeling Good & Living Great

Exercise. When you feel sad you may want to simply lay around in bed or on the sofa watching TV or eating comfort food. Yet, none of this is good for you. In fact, research shows that even a little physical activity can help lift your sorrow substantially. When you exercise you benefit from the release of positive endorphins. You improve circulation and increase your vitality. Exercise at this point doesn't have to be strenuous. Just moving about the house some more or going for a walk around your neighborhood can be enough to get you going.

Exercise can help in other ways. I remember a client of mine who was recovering from an illness and suffering from depression. Though he lived in sunny San Diego, he had not been outside for weeks. Finally, due to my suggestion, he went outside and took a short walk. When he got home he felt so good he went for a few more. When I saw him again for counseling he was like a changed man. The exercise, sunshine, and ocean breeze had brought a smile back to his face. "I was forgetting how much there was to still enjoy in life," he declared. Both exercise and remembering to enjoy the good things had helped him lift out of his sorrowful mood.

Talk. Talking about your loss and sorrow can be very helpful. People who experience loss often feel traumatized causing them to want to talk about their loss over and over again. Listening to someone share their story of the loss and trauma requires a great deal of patience and skill. Though people can get stuck in their trauma by retelling it too often, on a healthy level retelling a traumatic tale helps people break through denial. It also helps them let go and brings them insight, forgiveness, and peace.

Sometimes people who are not skilled at helping others with grief and trauma may not recognize the potential positive benefits of retelling the tale, and they may attempt to get others to shut up prematurely. As a counselor at times I would run into family members who would want me to hurry the grief process up so their loved ones would stop talking about the loss and get back to being "normal" again. More than once, I had to gently ask family members to be more patient with listening to the pain in their loved one's hearts. To their amazement, when they did so, their loved ones actually moved through the loss sooner because they were given permission to go deeper into their sorrow and fully feel their pain allowing them to release it that much sooner.

Book and Movie Therapy. Hands down there is one book I use to help others heal from a significant loss. It is the book *To Heal Again* by Rusty Burkus. Time and again I have seen men and women deeply touched by this book. The book is simply a short poem set to a series of beautiful pictures. Maybe it is the combination of the words and pictures that touches people so much helping them to deepen their experience of loss and grief until it can be replaced with acceptance, hope, and love. Other books that are helpful in dealing with sorrow include those that educate your logical mind regarding the stages of grief, and those filled with poems and meaningful phrases like the ones often found in sacred scriptures.

Feeling Good & Living Great

Movies can also be powerful tools to help educate people about how to cope with loss, depression, and grief in a healthy way. A few of my favorites are *An Unfinished Life* and *Off the Map*. (Note: to receive a free copy of some of these movie reviews look under the free gift section on my www.doctorlisalove.com web site). In *An Unfinished Life* viewers can readily see the price that is paid if they attempt to deny their pain. And, they can contrast this with healthier methods revealed in the film of how to face sorrow more head on. *Off the Map* provides excellent lessons for helping people coping with loss, especially those dealing with deep depression. *Off the Map* also focuses on the problem of male depression. Especially since men have a more difficult time admitting to sorrow and coping with loss, *Off the Map* is a wonderful film to see.

<u>Avoid Depression</u>. When sorrow does becomes depression it means you are failing to let go of something or someone you need to. And, it means you are engaging in a particular brand of irrational thinking that is usually catastrophic and absolute in nature. For example, you believe that you *should not* have lost what you have just lost. Or, you believe there is *no way* you can survive after having lost what you have. This "no way out" aspect of depression is what feeds the helplessness and hopelessness that can lead to suicidal thoughts and behaviors.

But, depression is more complex than this and actually involves other emotions besides just sorrow. For instance depression often comes from a sense of fatigue or simply feeling worn out in many or all aspects of your life. Instead of medicating yourself you might be better served by taking time to sufficiently rest before diving back into the hectic pace of life and the constant focus on doing over being. Confusion is also typically present with depression feeding your inability to see a way out of your current situation. Confusion adds to the sense of stagnation since you no longer comprehend how to survive, let alone thrive, from this point forward. And, depression frequently covers up anger that is being submerged because you are refusing to get angry, feel helpless if you do, or don't know who or what to be angry at and why!

To adequately treat depression you need to do more than simply medicate yourself. You need to rest so you have the energy to think. You need to meditate so you can breakthrough and get clarity and no longer languish in confusion. And, you need to get angry in the right way so you can reclaim the energy you need to push your life into a new direction. Then you will feel empowered enough to lift the anchors of your sadness and sorrow that have been holding you down so you can move into becoming a new you capable of attracting the joy and prosperity you are meant to.

More Tips to Manage Sorrow

1. Take the onset of sorrow and depression seriously.
2. Confront sorrow and depression right away.
3. Have a logical plan of action in place to help you cope with sorrow or depression if it emerges.

Feeling Good & Living Great

4. Avoid depressive routines like staying in bed, closing the curtains, and avoiding looking your best.
5. Don't isolate yourself. Stay in contact with family, friends, nature, and loved ones.
6. Practice smiling and surround yourself with humor (light-hearted people, funny movies, etc.).
7. Resist the temptation to talk in a depressed way.
8. Expand your awareness to include others who may need you because helping others can be a way to help yourself.

Sorrow Affirmations

1. Each and every day I am feeling my sorrow, learning its lessons, freeing myself from pain, and moving on.
2. More and more I am releasing that which needs to be released so I can attract something or someone new and more meaningful towards me.
3. I love knowing that this loss has the potential to open my heart to greater compassion for myself and others.
4. Here and now I use this sorrow to feel my remorse, gain insight into myself and others, and increase my capacity to love and be wise.

Sorrow Visualization

Healing Waters. Find a comfortable space where you can sit or lie down peacefully without being interrupted for at least twenty minutes. After you settle into the chair, bed, or sofa take a few deep breaths. As you breath out tell yourself, "Let go, relax." As you breath in tell yourself, "Renew, be my highest and best self." Continue to breathe, but shift your focus and gently bring into your awareness that which is making you feel sad. Notice any heaviness in your heart, slumping of your shoulders, or tendency to breathe at a shallow level. Don't try to change any of this, just notice it for now. Continue to recollect what is making you feel sad and allow yourself to experience that sadness more fully.

Next as you focus on your sadness notice any tears that emerge. Let the tears and sorrow flow from you. Experience any sense of helplessness, hopelessness, doubt, discouragement, or disappointment that may emerge. As you do so sense all of it moving down the front of your body as if you are releasing it into a river below. Let this river flow down to your feet and then allow it to flow away from you carrying all of your sadness with it.

Continue to see this river of sorrow flow away from you. Only as it does so imagine that the water is flowing over rocks and other elements found within the river. As your sorrow flows over these objects imagine that any negativity or pain is being cleansed and purified. See the waters of your sorrow becoming pure and crystalline reflecting the sun and sky above giving you a greater sense of clarity, perspective, and hope. Notice that as the sun above the river is warming the water, it is simultaneously warming your heart.

Eventually see the river of your sorrow pouring

out into a lake or ocean. As it touches this larger body of water notice how your sorrow is being replaced by an abundance of warmth and love. See and feel that warmth and love coming from the sun. As the sun continues to warm the lake and also your heart, imagine a vaporous mist rising up from the ocean forming a rain cloud overhead. As the rain cloud becomes full see it moving towards you. Once it is above you see and feel the rain pour down upon you imagining that as it does so that it is blessing you with love, light, hope, warmth, and healing. Conclude by experiencing yourself as revitalized and reenergized as you lift into the higher vibration of your soul.

Sorrow Bach Flowers

- Sudden Loss: Rescue Remedy, Star of Bethlehem
- Discouraged: Gentian
- Hopeless: Gorse
- Despairing: Sweet Chestnut

Shifting Anger Into Energy

Anger is perhaps the most frequently expressed emotion and the most misunderstood. You know you get angry. You may even know at times why you get angry. Yet, too often you may have no real understanding of what you are trying to accomplish with your anger beyond simply blowing off steam. And, because you don't understand what your anger is trying to reveal to you, it can frequently blow up your efforts to attract what you want because you fail to get angry in the right way. So, what is anger trying to teach you? Consider the following:

*Anger implores you to set boundaries
and establish a field of mutual respect.*

Gifts and Costs of Anger

You see most people rarely get angry unless they feel someone is disregarding and disrespecting their boundaries, needs, and wants. Anger then is asking you to pay attention to the following questions:

*Where do I feel misunderstood, disrespected,
and in danger at this moment?*

*What do I need to communicate to someone to help
me feel understood, respected, safe and secure?*

Anger like fear has a protective element to it. That need for protection is removed once you have a sense that others are attempting to understand and respect you. Part of being respected is knowing that you are free from others abuse. Because anger often slips into abuse (verbal, emotional, mental, physical), anger gets a bad rap. But, if you pay attention to what the early signals of anger are trying to teach you, then anger can quickly turn into a signal that a process of dialogue and communication needs to happen in order to create respect between you and other people. Ignore these signals and fail to enter into that healthy dialogue and here are some of the costs that can emerge when you don't handle your anger well:

1. A debilitated sense of self-worth and self-respect.
2. Resentment and anger from others when you mismanage your anger and resort to abuse.
3. A collapse into self-hatred, lethargy and possibly addictive and destructive behaviors.
4. Negative consequences to your health since anger tends to raise your blood pressure.
5. A collapsing of your boundaries if you do not know how to set them causing you to become involved in unhealthy relationships.

Levels Of Anger

Healthy Anger Zone — Lesson: Seek to Be Understood

1. Irritated — Engage through communication/dialogue.

Feeling Good & Living Great

2. Frustrated — Signal that you need distance/respect.
3. Exasperated — Reinforce need for distance/respect.

Average Anger Zone — Lesson: Enforce Boundaries

4. Resentful — Set boundaries to time out situation.
5. Angry — Stay in time out until cooled down.
6. Disgusted— Set more rigid boundaries if needed.

Unhealthy Anger Zone — Lesson: Restore Respect

7. Hateful — Work through desire to hurt/punish.
8. Furious — Get distance before you hurt/punish others.
9. Enraged — Avoid cruel counter-response.

    At the healthy levels anger shows up as irritation, frustration, and exasperation warning you that you are beginning to feel disrespected and need to set a boundary to preserve respect. And, it indicates that dialogue and compassionate communication need to take place. Though you may attempt to be patient and ignore what is going on if your anger continues it is best to communicate in an effective way what you are needing from the other person to feel understood, respected, and safe again. If you don't know how to communicate what you need, or the other person ignores you, exasperation may emerge. Now, your anger will likely show up as an emotional display through facial expressions, body language, gestures, and words that may even involve yelling or cursing behaviors.

Having descended to from the average levels of anger to the unhealthy ones it is now absolutely essential that you set a boundary and time out the discussion (usually by walking away) before it disintegrates even further into disgust or even hate. Hate is actually a deep feeling of hurt. You feel hurt that people, especially those you care about and love, don't respect you. After all, at one point they were probably the people you most counted on to protect you and offer support. At this point it is important to shift from working with anger to healing your sorrow especially since you may be forced to remove someone you once loved and cared for completely out of your life. If you don't do this your anger may continue to drop to the destructive levels as fury and rage.

Next to learning to communicate your needs effectively, anger is best managed if you cultivate a sense of spiritual self-worth. I am reminded of a scene from the classic film *To Kill A Mockingbird*. In this film the amazing actor Gregory Peck portrays a lawyer, Atticus Finch, who is defending a black man charged with raping a white woman. Set in the south in the 1950's when prejudice was extremely high, Atticus leaves the home of his client only to run into a white man who threatens him and spits on his face as Atticus is attempting to get into his car.

Calmly, yet very firmly, Atticus stares back at the man. Then he pulls out his handkerchief, wipes off the spit, walks around the man, gets in his truck, and drives away. As he does so the white man is clearly ashamed.

This scene is powerful for a number of reasons. At one level Atticus says to the man non-verbally, "I'm not going to stoop to your level and act in such an undignified way." But, at another level Atticus demonstrates that he is a man worthy of respect and people who respect themselves avoid indulging in such degrading behaviors. And, by treating the man in a respectful way even when he didn't deserve it, Atticus reveals that treating others with respect makes it more likely to illicit respect from them in return.

You see the more genuine and heart-felt respect you generate from others, the more they will come to admire you and possibly even offer you love and protection. In the movie *To Kill a Mockingbird* this was especially demonstrated through the character of Boo Radley, a ridiculed shy recluse who Atticus also treats well, who in return ended up saving the lives of Atticus's children. The genuine respect of others can also bring you a greater sense of security because you are more likely to have people assist you when you need it the most. Feeling secure in turn helps you remain calm allowing you to manage your anger and cope more effectively in a world that at times can seem overwhelmingly harsh and difficult.

Main Methods for Shifting Anger

<u>Meditate</u>. Long before anger slips into the average or unhealthy levels you can learn to catch and eliminate it

early on when it is only a minor irritation or frustration through the practice of meditation. Face it, it is hard to be irritated with someone whom you feel at peace with! One of the reasons people start to feel irritated is because their nerves are getting frazzled. Taking a time out right away when you begin to feel upset and then deliberately taking twenty to thirty minutes to center and calm yourself through relaxation or meditation helps counter this. Unfortunately, in our super fast paced world we often don't give people the option to relax and meditate when things are beginning to bubble over let alone when they are reaching the boiling point. Instead, we encourage people to suck it up and keep on moving forward even if this forces them into the average and unhealthy levels of anger where they will implode or explode.

Imagine what a different world we would have if this were not the case. Wouldn't it be a wonderful thing if whenever people started to feel tense we asked them to cool off, relax, and meditate? In many ways this is what we do when we ask children to take a time out. Yet, too often our media and workplaces do not enforce this same time out philosophy. Instead, we, and they, advocate, watch, listen to and attract scenarios where people amplify their irritation into increased anger by trying to out do one another through escalated levels of hostility and even violence. Relaxation and meditation are a wonderful antidote to this and something we can all engage in to help attract more peace into our world.

<u>Set Boundaries</u>. Especially if you tend to suppress

your anger you need to learn how to set more protective boundaries in your life. One of the reasons people fail to set boundaries is because at a young age when they were vulnerable and helpless they were unable to protect themselves. When the people they relied upon for nurturance and protection (parents, siblings, religious leaders, teachers) ended up abusing them instead of protecting them, they developed what has been called a "learned helplessness" response making them passive and unaware of how deprived they are of protection, love, and respect. Being able to counter this helplessness is one reason learning how to set healthy boundaries is important.

To set a boundary you may need to retreat to a safe place like your home, religious gathering place, somewhere in nature, your room, or a friend's residence where you can sort things out. From there you can both think about and visualize setting boundaries in your life. To set boundaries some people may encourage you to imagine yourself surrounded by white light. Others may ask you to visualize a force field around yourself that is capable of repelling the negativity of others.

These tools are useful, but they have to be followed up by using your logical mind and not just your motivational mind. That's because just imagining you are setting a boundary is not enough. Logically, you may also need to think about who you can turn to and where you can go to get protection and support (domestic violence shelters for example). And, you may need to engage your intuitive mind to help you discern whether the people you are attracting in your life are really friends or enemies.

Forgive. Forgiveness has always been a major part of my life. I would much rather forgive, focus on what is positive, move on with my life and feel good. But, experience has also revealed that though forgiveness has it's place some times it is not always a good thing to forgive and forget! Examine those two words for a moment and you will find that they convey a notion of for-giving and for-getting. In other words, they demonstrate a need for reciprocity that allows a certain level of balance and karmic adjustment to come into play. (I give to you and you give to me. I get from you and you get from me. There we're even). Even the Christian pacifist Jesus said, "Go and sin no more," when he forgave people encouraging them not to forget, but to learn the lessons of how to stop being hurtful to others.

Some people also like to point out that Jesus said to "turn the other cheek." But, that isn't saying, "Ok, hit me again right here." It could symbolize turning your head to show the person another perspective and then saying to them metaphorically, "I understand you see it this way, but here is another way to look at it you may not have realized before." As the other person sees that there is another perspective they may develop empathy for your pain and circumstances motivating them to not hurt others in the same way again.

Take Responsibility. If you are someone prone to exploding your anger and abusing others it is absolutely essential that you take responsibility for the impact your negatively expressed anger is having on yourself and others. Sadly, many abusive people are experts at doing everything they can to get off the hook for their abuse. They may even try to get others to believe it is their fault they are being abused. For example, children who are abused verbally, physically, and sexually are frequently told by the abuser that they deserved the abuse. Remember the saying, "This is going to hurt me more than it hurts you?" Suddenly, a minor infraction, like eating a cookie without permission, is justification for the child being slapped, hit with a paddle, or beaten with a belt or whip. And, while the child is being abused in this horrible way, the abuser even makes it seem like it is the abuser, not the child, who is getting hurt in the encounter. Ridiculous!

This bizarre reversal of responsibility creates a helpless feeling in the child as she grows up making her unfortunately more subject to being abused in the future by others because she will now gladly take responsibility (accept the blame) for things that aren't even her fault! ("Oh, did I forget to buy you some coffee today? Ok, I guess I deserve your verbal and physical abuse now"). One way to avoid this is simple. Anytime anyone resorts to verbal, physical, or sexual abuse, *they* are the one's responsible for having resorted to abuse as a means of handling their anger. Put bluntly, abuse is *never* an option! Never! Resorting to abuse and violence is always a sign that someone has failed to manage her anger in a conscious and healthy way by learning to set boundaries and ask for the respect and support of others in a more spiritual way!

Taking responsibility also means healing your core hurts (a phrase used by abuse expert Steven Stosny, Ph.D.). In his book *You Don't Have to Take it Anymore*, Stosny defines core hurts as those areas within you that make you feel bad about yourself. These cause you to feel inadequate, unimportant, and disregarded. Over time these turn into an inner sense of shame that is covered up with blame and abusive behaviors if you are not careful. Only as you face your core hurts, cultivate empathy and spiritual values, and learn to cope more effectively with your feelings of insecurity, inadequacy, and pain, will taking responsibility become easy for you.

<u>*Don't Tolerate Abuse*</u>. Violence is the worst expression of anger and sadly it has been a part of humanity's legacy for as long as humanity has been around. Violence does not always display itself as verbal, physical, and sexual abuse. It can also manifest as a need to control others. Violence is rarely the result of low self-esteem. Rather, violent people tend to have too much self-esteem, mostly at an egotistical level. Lundy Bancroft in his book *Why Does He Do That?* reveals how violence itself is an act of entitlement since only entitled people feel they have the right to control, humiliate, and intimidate others through abuse.

Regretfully, many people even admire violent behavior. Video games, television shows, movies, music, talk radio, porn, are increasingly saturated with stories that legitimize violence as a tool to get what you want in life.

Feeling Good & Living Great

Some police agencies, various political and legal systems, and even some religious teachings also feed the notion that violence and abuse are acceptable. The fact that we have a world wide mentally that views violence as a viable method for solving problems makes the shift from ego to soul difficult. Sadly, as long as violence is condoned in this way, the people who resort to violence will feel little to zero shame for resorting to their abusive behaviors meaning they will have no motivation for change.

Fortunately, there is a growing trend to send a message that no one is entitled to abuse others. As this message takes hold humans will insist that violence be removed from the minds, emotions and actions of people, as well as from places of work, political arenas, households, and in all forms of media. In fact, one of the best things we can do is to insist that in all areas of our lives violence is no longer acceptable. And, we need to insist that people who are abusive enter programs that teach them to drop their entitled attitudes and distorted thinking patterns that lead them to control and abuse others in the first place. Finally, we need to insist on greater civility in all areas of our lives to counter the trend to be profane and abusive on radio, television, the workplace, and worst of all within the home.

More Tips to Manage Anger

1. Speak up immediately and set limits on anger that becomes abusive. Stop accepting abuse of any kind

whenever it emerges. Let people know that it is not acceptable in your world.
2. Stop confusing control and abuse with love. Remember love never hurts. If someone you love is hurting you get support, leave if you have to, and find ways to rebuild your self-worth so you have more control of your destiny and soul.
3. No one can thrive in an atmosphere of abuse. If someone does not know how to nourish your soul, actively repel that person and seek to attract healthier and more nourishing people to you.
4. If you have a legacy of being in controlling and abusive relationships remember to be cautious regarding the people you attract. Until you have managed to stay away from abusive people for a period of a few years (maybe longer) you are still in danger of falling back into your old pattern where you will be vulnerable to attracting people who are not good for you.

Anger Affirmations

1. Here and now I am increasingly committed to creating a world that teaches others to handle anger in a respectful and non-violent way.
2. More and more I learn to catch and handle my anger effectively when it is only at the level of mild irritation or frustration.
3. Each and every day I learn and apply something useful that helps me improve my self-worth and in turn de-

mands that others treat me in a respectful way.
4. I love knowing that I can set boundaries and earn the respect of others in a compassionate, forceful, non-violent and even loving way.

Anger Visualization

Into the Light. Some time ago I was subjected to a situation that made me feel grossly and unfairly treated. Naturally, I was angry and being a strong believer in law of attraction methods I sought out some popular CD's for working with anger through the method of visualization. To my great disappointment the CD's I listened to advocated the same old tired approach of directing your anger at another person by seeing them disintegrate, blow up, or in some other way be destroyed.

Worried that by using these kind of visual images I might be setting up a magnetic field of violent anger and increase the odds of violence being attracted to another person, I decided to make up my own visualization. The following visualization borrows from the Hercules myth of slaying the nine headed hydra where Hercules discovers that whenever he cuts off one head three more grow in it's place. Finally, he gives up this approach and in humility raises the hydra into the light where the immortal and spiritual head of the hydra is revealed.

Again find a comfortable space where you can sit or lie down peacefully without being interrupted for at least twenty minutes. After you settle into the chair, bed, or sofa take a few deep breaths. As you breathe in tell yourself, "Renew, be my highest and best self." As you breathe out tell yourself, "Let go, relax." Continue to breathe and as you do so shift your focus and bring your attention to whatever (or whoever) is making you angry. Now get a sense of how this anger feels in your body. Notice any areas that feel hot, irritated, or constricted. For now just make a mental note of where they are.

As you become increasingly aware of your anger imagine that every incident that has created your irritation, anger, or rage is turning into a head of a horrible dragon like beast. Notice as you stand in front of this beast if you feel timid and afraid, or aggressive and ready to strike. For now don't act on your impulses, just observe what is there. As you continue to watch the heads of the beast multiply do your best to lift your attention away from them. Instead, notice a small golden globe evolving into a warm sun over the many heads of the beast (and the anger the heads of the beast represent). Continue to experience this sun as growing in power, heat, and intensity. Know that this sun is filled with a higher spiritual vibration that carries within it the wisdom of how best to handle the situation confronting you. Do not attempt to intuit or understand what this wisdom may be about. Just keep your attention on the growing sun and the beast below it.

Next, imagine that the heat from the sun above is starting to consume (exhaust, melt down, or burn up) the beast below. As it does see how the coarse, angry, and raging aspects of the beast are diminished. Eventually, in the center of the beast see the immortal spiritual self of the beast emerge. See that spiritual self taking the beast over until it has zero power to harm or destroy because it is now vibrating at a more spiritual level.

As this process ends turn your attention away from the beast and focus on the sun itself. Enter into a silent communication with the light of the sun. As you do so allow that light to fill your intuitive and logical minds with insight and wisdom regarding how to handle anger more effectively in your life. Conclude by allowing your mind to go completely quiet and simply experience the warmth of the sun as it dissolves any areas of tension or anger in your body. When you come out of the meditation be sure to write your experiences down.

Anger Bach Flowers

- Giving into Others' Anger: Agrimony
- Feeling Irritated: Beech
- Explosive Tendencies: Cherry Plum
- Impatient With Self and Others: Impatiens
- Self Hatred: Pine
- Overly Aggressive and Domineering: Vine
- Resentment: Willow

Shifting Jealousy Into Fulfillment

Feeling Good & Living Great

Jealousy is perhaps one of the most difficult emotions to understand and is often considered the most demonic. Who hasn't heard of the "green eyed monster?" No other emotion evokes the monster image so quickly. No wonder it is difficult to imagine that jealousy could have one gift to offer you, let alone several. But, it does!

*Jealousy helps you get clear about
what you most desire in life.*

Gifts and Costs of Jealousy

In many ways jealousy only emerges when you fear you will not receive what you want in life, or will lose what you have attracted to you. As these fears mix in with anger you can feel threatened and upset with those you believe may not give you what you want, or take what you have away from you. That is why jealousy often results in controlling and hysterical behaviors that end up turning others off in such a dramatic way. Asking these questions when you feel jealous is important then:

*Where do I lack the faith and insight
to help me get what I really want?*

*What do I need to let go of so I can better
attract what Spirit really wants for me?*

Often people who get jealous are not even clear

about what they are jealous about. Consider this example. You are at a party and start to feel jealous when your girlfriend is involved in an interaction with a man across the room. You feel jealous, but that doesn't necessarily mean you are afraid of losing her. It may mean you are afraid of losing power and control over her. Or, she may be violating your ideas about how "your woman" should interact with others. Her being too far across the room may even be triggering off your issues about being disconnected and abandoned, especially if you have a history of losing people you feel close to. Getting clear about what is causing your jealousy is important. And, failing to get clear can hurt you as seen in some of the costs below:

1. An inability to get clear about what makes you content so you can attract greater joy, love, and prosperity.
2. Holding on to people and things out of fear and control causing you to cling to people and items that you would be better off letting go of.
3. Getting overly caught up in attracting stuff to feel good about yourself and then spending all your time and energy defending and protecting it so no one will take it away from you.
4. An inability to appreciate what you do have so you can live more fully in the moment in a state of joy, peace, and contentment.
5. A continued distortion of reality that causes you to debase your spiritual nature causing you to attract people and things that ultimately are not good for you.

Feeling Good & Living Great

Levels Of Jealousy

Healthy Jealousy Zone — Lesson: Clarify What You Want

1. Desirous — Get clear about what you are wanting.
2. Insecure — Reaffirm you can attract what you want.
3. Annoyed — Communicate needs clearly to others.

Average Jealousy Zone — Lesson: Cultivate Faith

4. Jealous — Examine irrational assumptions.
5. Covetous — Avoid plotting and vengeful thoughts.
6. Deceitful — Remain truthful about your intentions.

Unhealthy Jealousy Zone — Lesson: Reassure Yourself

7. Obsessive — Obsess on positives not negatives.
8. Paranoid — Broaden your perspective.
9. Panicky — Let go and let God. Trust!

    At the healthy levels taking time to get clear about what your jealousy is triggering off helps you get a deeper understanding of your wants. In the example of the man and his girlfriend, what the man may have really wanted was to have his girlfriend pay more attention to him and help him feel more welcome in the room. Or, he might have wanted her to follow some relationship protocol guidelines that would help him feel more comfortable. For example: Let him introduce her first to people he knows. Ask her to help him feel more confident so he can overcome his shyness by standing by him as they mingle with others. Request that she send him reassuring signals that she is not abandoning him when she is interacting with someone by looking over at him now and then. Or, making sure she is not gone away too long.

It is also important at the healthy levels that as you get more clear about what your want that you communicate these needs and wants effectively to people around you. The man in the example above could say something like, "Honey, I'm a little anxious being here. There are a lot of people I don't know and I am worried about making a good impression. Can you just stay a little closer to me and help me relax?" That's certainly a lot better than stuffing feelings and then letting them out in an abusive way later by saying something like, "You bitch! Why did you leave me alone in the room? Who was that guy anyway? Don't ever talk to him again!" These reactions are what give jealousy such a bad rap. They are also what make jealous people seem irrational, controlling and at times even abusive.

When you lose touch with your ability to identify and communicate your needs life becomes more difficult and you start to slip into the average levels of jealousy. Here you start to lose confidence that you can attract what you are meant to. You may even resort to lying, cheating, and stealing in an attempt to make your wishes come true. Having sunk to these covetous and deceitful levels you are in further danger of covering up your deceptive and hurtful ways by getting defensive because you don't want to be held accountable for your manipulative behaviors.

Slipping into the unhealthy zones, obsession may even kick in causing you to go to any lengths to get what you want. Blackmail, hypocrisy, deception, playing others against each other, double standards, lies — whatever works. At this point you don't care since you have dropped completely away from the higher levels of the soul into the level of your ego. Like hungry wolves you may be hell bent on feeding your desires no matter what.

Naturally, other people may get upset over this. As they uncover your deceptive, immoral, and hypocritical behaviors they may even want revenge. As others direct their mounting anger towards you, jealousy can drop to full blown paranoia. To protect yourself from the attacks of others the projection and blame game may be used to deflect others away from your flaws or finding out what you are really up to. If these tactics don't work paranoia can become panic as you now realize you can run but there is really no place to hide. The end result? You lose everything you attempted to attract, and possibly more!

Main Methods for Shifting Jealousy

<u>*Don't Feed Irrational Beliefs*</u>. More than any other emotion jealousy is based upon a host of irrational beliefs. Some of these beliefs include: "I must always get what I want. If I don't get what I want I will be miserable. Other people have what I want and I can never have what they

do. The people I love must always love me and can never have loving feelings for anyone else. If the person I love pays attention to someone else it is catastrophic. I can't ever lose what I have. Losing is the end of the world making me a loser in the eyes of myself and others."

These beliefs cloud and distort your thinking and even cause you to think in chaotic and rigid ways. A vicious circle is created where your jealousy unwittingly prevents anything good from being attracted to you. For example, truly loving people will naturally be loving towards others. But, their acting in a loving way towards others doesn't mean they will leave you or don't love you. Take time then to be sure your perceptions of others are correct. Because if you are distorting them you will only sabotage the love they genuinely feel for you since you continue to allow your instinctual mind to hold on to distorted beliefs.

Manage Your Projections. Over the years Tim had contacted me regarding his various relationships. Early on he had been left by his girlfriend for another man. Though he was shaken, eventually he moved on with another woman. But, soon this relationship was also in trouble because now he was always jealous and afraid another man would take her away from him. Ironically, because of his jealous and controlling behaviors she ended up doing just that. As he started his third relationship I focused on helping him resolve his jealously only to discover something new — that over the years he had been cheating on his girlfriends with other women.

Feeling Good & Living Great

With this new information I realized my client was doing something a lot of people do. He was measuring other people according to how he behaved himself. Since he was frequently talking, flirting, and even having sex with other women, he assumed his girlfriends must be doing the same. But, something deeper was going on here. As my client looked into his true desires he confessed that he didn't really want just one woman. Instead, he wanted to be admired by lots of women, and in turn he wanted to be certain that they would want only him. Why? Because he figured if he had lots of women wanting him, and only him, he would never risk rejection.

Uncovering at last his true desires I was better able to help Tim challenge his irrational assumptions, especially of trying to make it through life without ever feeling rejected again. As I helped him move beyond his irrational beliefs, get back into integrity, and clean up his negative karma (created by cheating on the women he was with) he eventually healed. And, as he changed his behaviors he even learned how to win the admiration and love of women through being a loving and honest person.

Have Faith. A primary reason jealousy becomes such a major problem is because you don't have faith that what you are really meant to have will come to you. Anger, fear, and doubt kick in making you impatient and demanding. Like a child having a temper tantrum your ego "wants what it wants when it wants it." The more demanding and impatient you get, the more jealous and upset you feel that what you want may not come your way.

All of this is countered by faith, especially a faith that what Spirit really wants for you will be attracted to you. You simply need to stay in touch with your intuitive mind to continually discern what it is that Spirit is trying to get you to attract. Usually, Spirit wants you to attract spiritual values and soul qualities that will help you live a more joyful life. When you are in the state of joy you will in turn experience greater contentment making jealousy nearly impossible.

<u>Learn to Appreciate</u>. Jealousy comes about primarily due to a sense of lack. When you focus on what you don't have instead of what you do have, discontent sets in. I remember a time when I injured my arm and developed a frozen shoulder that prevented me from lifting my arm more than a few inches up or down and side to side. It was a horribly painful experience, though thankfully after one year of physical therapy my arm returned to normal. Attempting to cope with the chronic pain, I would go to sleep being thankful for little things like having food in my mouth, a bed to sleep in, a roof over my head, at least one good arm that was still working, and so much more. By focusing on the positive I was better able to keep my thoughts and feelings on a positive level.

Appreciation is also useful by helping you acknowledge all the baby steps you make in life. I frequently tell my clients about the movie *Touching the Void*. This true story is about a young man who takes a fall over a cliff into a deep crevasse. On the fall he breaks his leg. Alone at the top of a mountain and left for dead, amazingly, he survives, climbs down the mountain on his own, and makes it back home. The secret to his success? 50 feet at a time.

Instead of focusing on getting all the way back down the mountain, which would have rapidly put him into overwhelm and despair, he concentrated on just seeing if he could move 50 feet in front of him. In a similar way if you focus on too big a goal and allow yourself to get overwhelmed jealousy is likely to emerge because you will no longer believe you can get what you want. By putting your attention on appreciating what you have and focusing on how you can move along one step at a time, jealousy diminishes allowing you to stay open to the realms of inspiration that can show you how to keep moving forward in a positive direction.

Get Clear About Your Wants and Don't Wants. I once counseled a man who was very jealous of other people who were wealthy. On the surface he appeared to desire wealth. But, at the same time he didn't want to take any of the steps that would help him become a wealthy individual. For example, he didn't want to get a job where making a lot of money was probable. He didn't want to have to work long hours. He didn't like the hassle of managing a lot of money, and so forth. Thankfully, as he became more clear about all of this, his jealousy diminished, and he learned to appreciate his life as it was.

Though getting clear about what you really want is important, you need to communicate those wants to others in a confident and assertive way. It is also important to discern if those you are talking to are really able to give you what you desire. Plus, being persistent and loving in your communication is important increasing the odds for getting what you from others.

More Tips to Manage Jealousy

1. What are you really wanting?
2. How confident are you that you will get it?
3. If you are afraid of not getting what you want how often do you blame other people for this?
4. How might you be avoiding your faults by projecting them onto other people?
5. If you were 100% responsible for getting what you want how might you change knowing this?
6. If you are 100% responsible for learning from your mistakes and correcting your own flaws, what must you do?
7. How can you commit to admitting your weaknesses and setting up a plan of action to change your thoughts, feelings, and behaviors so you will have these weaknesses no more?

Jealousy Affirmations

1. Here and now I get clear on my wants and don't wants.
2. More and more I cultivate the confidence and knowledge I need to more effectively get what I want.

3. Each and every day I improve my capacity to communicate my desires to others in a loving and effective way so they are more inclined to support me in my goals and dreams.
4. I love knowing that I can appreciate what I already have in life feeling happy and secure in who I am and with what life brings me as I strive to attract more of what Spirit wants for me from this day forward.

Jealousy Visualization

Temple of the Sun. Make sure you will not be interrupted for at least a period of twenty minutes. Then, assume a comfortable position, either sitting or lying down. Make sure you are physically relaxed, but not to the point of total relaxation. Now, close your eyes and imagine that you are in front of a pyramid with four sets of stairs moving upward towards a temple with a small room overhead. In that small room is something you very much want, such as a relationship, financial security, a more rewarding job, a child, and so forth. Even though getting to that room from the bottom of the pyramid may seem difficult, experience your longing to reach the temple until the desire to get there seems almost irresistible.

Now, descend up the first set of stairs noticing that it contains twenty steps. These steps are related to your instinctual mind. Each step is labeled with an irrational belief, either the same belief on every step, or different ones existing on more than one step. As you place your foot on each step imagine the irrational beliefs dissolving and greater clarity emerging regarding what you want, and what Spirit wants for you.

Having finished your first climb up the pyramid notice that you are standing on a plateau. Rest for awhile. Then, engage your motivational mind and put your attention again on the small room in the temple overhead. Set the intent to get crystal clear about what is waiting for you there. As you climb the next twenty stairs allow that clarity to emerge. Putting your foot on each of the twenty stairs, notice how your motivation to reach the small room overhead and get what you want is intensifying.

Reaching the next plateau prepare yourself to journey up the third flight of twenty stairs. Know as you put your foot on each step your logical mind will reveal something practical you need to do to ensure that you can in fact attract what is waiting for you in the upper room.

By the time you reach the third plateau notice to your amazement that instead of feeling tired after climbing sixty stairs, you feel radiant and energized. This time as you continue your ascent, let your intuitive mind come into play. See it as a golden ball of sunlight dissolving all limitations within you, mentally, emotionally, and physically. Notice as you climb these last twenty steps that you feel lighter, freer, and more filled with confidence, joy, and energy. And, you are feeling increasingly pulled into the direction of the room that contains your desires in an almost effortless way.

Reaching the last plateau, you are filled with anticipation as you finally stand in front of the small room that contains what you wish for. See the door to the room slowly opening. As it does so see the walls of the room collapse. All that remains is an angelic being holding or standing next to what you desire. Just as you reach out for it suddenly what you most desire disappears. Regardless of having lost it for now, you notice that you are being filled with joy and surrounded by light. Standing within that light allow the room, the stairs, and the temple to dissolve. Transported back to where you are now, realize that whether you do or do not have what you desire right now joy, love, light, and peace can still reside within you. Close by sending gratitude to Spirit for this realization.

Jealousy Bach Flowers

- Feeling Superior: Beech
- Possessive: Chicory
- Jealous & Suspicious: Holly
- Feeling Inferior: Larch
- Overly Concerned for Others: Red Chestnut
- Desiring Perfection to Feel Accepted: Rock Water
- Obsessive Thoughts: White Chestnut
- Envy and Resentment: Willow

Shifting Happiness Into Joy

Feeling Good & Living Great

Of all the feelings happiness is probably the one that most people consider good. True, happiness can be beneficial, but like all the other feeling states it can have its drawbacks, a fact you will soon discover. But, when happiness serves you it does so in the following ways:

*Happiness lightens you up and fuels you
with energy so you can move forward.*

Gifts & Costs of Happiness

Not surprisingly when you feel happy you tend to feel fulfilled. Happiness helps you to feel optimistic and brings you a feeling of contentment and inner peace so that you feel good about yourself and your life regardless of the outer appearance of your world. When you need to feel happy the following questions can help:

*How can I get back in touch with what gives me
pleasure and cultivate more of it in my life?*

*How can I laugh, smile, and feel more at choice
regarding how I live in this present moment?*

Though many things can make you happy from the level of the soul, happiness is connected more closely to the realm of joy. Joy is more about what's in it for everyone and not so much what's in it just for yourself. Joy orients you more towards giving than getting. Even when you have very little in a material way there is always something you can give, be it a smile, a hug, a word of encouragement, or love. In that way they will avoid the pitfalls of happiness that follow:

1. A shift towards a self-indulgent and egotistical quest for happiness that benefits yourself alone.
2. An entitled attitude that you should be happy all the time no matter what.
3. Pretending to be happy while denying other emotions that you may need to confront and heal.
4. Living a life of excess that is mostly superficial and shallow in nature.
5. Not understanding that sometimes unhappiness (in the form of challenges and difficulties) can be good for you when it helps you grow spiritually.
6. Using happiness as an excuse to insist that others always feel and act positive as a means to help you escape unpleasant emotions.

Levels Of Happiness

Healthy Happiness Zone — Lesson: Give Selflessly

Serene — Live in joy because life is about giving.
Content — Appreciate life no matter what.
Pleased — Be happy with what you have.

Average Happiness Zone — Lesson: Benefit Self & Others

4. Happy — Be glad but stay aware of others.
5. Desirous — Be cautious about the need to want more.
6. Craving — Monitor the tendency to become addicted.

Unhealthy Happiness Zone — Lesson: Stop Being Selfish

7. Hedonistic — Remember others' needs matter too.
8. Manic — Expand perspective of what's important.
9. Satiated — Remove chronic discontentment traits.

One of the major attributes of the healthy level is that of joy. Have you ever noticed that someone can talk about being happy versus unhappy, but there is no word in the English language for being unjoyful? That is because joy brings about a state of serenity or peace, which is based upon contentment. Instead of looking out at your world as if there is always something you lack, you appreciate fully what you have. Feeling pleased is similar to the state of joy, but is a step below because joy comes about through service and helping others. Feeling pleased happens more when you feel things are going your way. The question is are they going your way for the benefit of yourself alone, or your way because you are joyously attracting it to you for the purpose of making a contribution to the world?

As you drop to the average happiness levels, your desire to be happy is now mixed and feeling good is increasingly about your ability to satisfy your external desires, instead of your ability to cultivate spiritual values and be of service to others. Happiness becomes more about having things go your way. The more things go your way the better you feel. That is precisely why people have made a cult out of happiness acting as if it is the only feeling you should have. This is good so long as your life is going in a way that is ultimately good for you in the long run. But, when your happiness becomes important at the expense of the happiness of others, happiness turns more and more into a craving and even an addiction.

That's why as happiness enters the average levels and drops even further into the unhealthy levels people begin to justify lying, cheating, and stealing to ensure they get their happiness fix. Happiness becomes a form of gluttony causing them to resort to anything (drugs, adrenal rush activities, sexual escapades, alcohol addictions, shopping binges, money deals and more) to feel happy or good. In short, happiness turns into hedonism.

The more you get your way the more you insist on having to get your way all the time. Mania can be the result as you insist on staying happy to avoid all other feeling states. But, since you now use your happiness to suppress all other emotions (which also have value), eventually you can experience happiness burnout as you become satiated in a happiness pursuit that has really become a reflection of just how unhappy you have become!

Thus, happiness becomes a danger when your ego buys into the belief that it should get whatever it wants, whenever it wants, without restraint, or thought of the costs it may have upon yourself or others in the long run.

Feeling Good & Living Great

It also becomes a problem when you buy into the belief that you should always feel happy, and that not feeling happy is somehow not good. These are irrational beliefs that have fed many law of attraction teachings that emphasize that it is fine to indulge yourself at all times as if you will never suffer any consequences. Happiness then becomes a disorder that leads to long term suffering. A lot of this is being seen today as people begin to experience the drawbacks of their misguided happiness pursuits.

Main Methods for Cultivating Happiness

Smile. It's a fact, when you smile you feel better about the world around you. On numerous occasions when I find myself feeling fatigued or resistant to a task I practice grinning from ear to ear to lift my mood. I might even practice singing out loud to music that is particularly uplifting and motivating. I have also been known to say to myself, "Up, up, up!" while smiling and throwing my arms up into the air to get the energy moving in an upwards instead of a downwards motion.

And, here is a particularly fun exercise I learned from a meditation teacher. When you wake up in the morning instead of saying to yourself, "Oh no, I need to face another day" jump out of bed and yell out loud, "Yipee!" or "Yahoo!" Yes, you may feel silly doing this. but you might also break into hysterical laughter. You can even practice doing this in front of others. In fact, one morning I shocked everyone in my networking group by starting the meeting with a leap into the air yelling out loud "Yahoo!" like a crazy person. Even though it was 7:00 am and everyone was a little bleary eyed, after my hysterical behavior nearly everyone was laughing so hard the energy charged up the room for the full ninety minute meeting. The point is if you don't feel happy, fake it until you make it. Because by setting the intention to be happy, you might just feel happy after all.

Cultivate Gratitude. When you feel unhappy about events in your life, a major way to lighten your mood is through the attitude of gratitude. Why does gratitude work? Because it helps refuel you, puts you into a positive space, and brings you the energy you need to cope with the circumstances you are faced with. It can even heal you at all levels, something I learned in a powerful way that year my arm was injured.

In fact, as I shared before when talking about my frozen shoulder, I believe gratitude heals pain as well. Why? Because as I was counting my blessings when lying in bed filled with pain, my mind felt soothed, my emotions calmed down, my breathing became deeper and more steady, and positive endorphins were flooding into my body. All of this in turn increased the capacity for my immune system to function better, which ultimately helped my arm to heal faster.

Laugh. Just as smiling helps to lighten your mood, laughter raises your disposition. Laughter also brings oxygen deep into your body helping to revitalize you. And, a really good belly laugh can help shake negativity out of your system. That's why one of the best ways to cheer yourself and someone else up is through laughing together. There are a variety of ways you can do this — crack jokes, share funny stories, watch comedies, be silly together. Just do what you can to lighten the mood, even if you laugh so hard together you cry at the end.

Laughter has an additional benefit in that it helps you detach from your problems. Comedy is really based upon seeing the irony or paradox of various situations. Comedy relies heavily on surprise or bringing about something unexpected. It helps you see both sides of a situation, lightens the mood, and helps you put your difficulties in perspective so you don't take them so seriously anymore. As you help others to lighten up you might even try this exercise with them. Simply sit next to them and fake some laughter for awhile. At first your fake guffaws will seem awkward. But, the more the two of you practice laughing together, and the more silly the whole thing seems, the more likely both of you will start genuinely laughing. In fact, that laughter may even become uncontrollable. And, when you are done laughing you may both wonder, "What were we so unhappy about?" It just won't seem important somehow anymore.

Feel Good Tool Kit. When you are not feeling happy one of the things you can do is build a "feel good tool kit." In this tool kit you put as many items as possible that will bring you happiness in the long run. What do you put in your "feel good tool kit?" Items like: 1) Visualizing happy scenarios you want to manifest in your life.

2) Surrounding yourself more with loving and supportive people. 3) Shoring up your existing friendships and intimate relationships so you build stronger and more loving bonds. 4) Filling your desire mind with thoughts of courage, health, hope, peace, and joy. 5) Engaging in exercise so you can flood your body with positive endorphins. 6) Getting absorbed in a cause bigger than yourself. 7) Acknowledging and working through various feeling states that prevent you from shifting towards happiness.

8) Eating healthier foods so you increase the vibratory rate of your body, mind, and Spirit. 9) Learning to cope with or transform more effectively negative people and events and, if you can't do this walking away from them. 10) Forgetting about your own happiness and working to bring a little more happiness into the lives of others. 12) Surrounding yourself with uplifting movies, music, books, and audio books that help you lift your vibration into a more positive state. 12) Getting a life by learning to enjoy nature, people, cultural events, uplifting ideas, and more! 13) Praying. 14) Meditating. 15) Creating. 16) Put your additional ideas here.

Love. Love connects you to others. It supports, nourishes, encourages, and uplifts you. The more love you attract into your life, the happier you tend to feel. That's why learning to love, being surrounded by loving people, and tapping into the eternal source of love, which is Spirit, is so important to feeling happy in this world. A good way to begin to attract love into your life is by setting an intention to love and be loved in return.

Feeling Good & Living Great

But, just setting an intention isn't enough. You need to know *how* to love others. One powerful way is through spending time together. Years ago I was passing by a church and saw the following billboard. "How do children spell love? T-I-M-E ." As you spend time with those you love focus on being sure that they end up really feeling and experiencing your love. Take time to make sure they feel connected, appreciated, and respected by you when you are with them. Ask if they feel that you really seeing and getting them when you are together. And, show them that you are concerned with helping them cultivate their unique talents and gifts so they can share them lovingly others on this Earth.

Love also has an element of "being there." People who have experienced abandonment in life were typically let down at crucial stages of their development (early childhood and adulthood). Not having people be there for you when you need them destroys trust and the feeling of connection that comes about when you are loved. When you are willing to "be there" for others it means you are wiling to give them your time, money, attention, skills, energy, even life because you truly love them. So, to make others, and yourself happy, take time to love and be there for them. Then others may be there to love, cherish, take time for and be there for you in return.

More Tips for Happiness

1. Practice random acts of kindness by doing nice things

for others just because it gives you pleasure to do so.
2. Appreciate others by finding something about them that you enjoy, brings you pleasure, or you admire.
3. Emphasize your areas of commonality instead of difference. Remember love is a great way to unite others. Though love respects and appreciates differences, it is always looking for common ground.
4. Help other people vibrate their feelings to a higher level. Remember all feelings can be either positive or negative. When you interject love into any feeling state, you lift it up, activate the spiritual levels, and attract positive resolutions into your life and the lives of those around you.
5. Be good to yourself as required. Remember to stay "well-full." Take time to love and nourish yourself especially as you hook up to Spirit and allow yourself to tap into the realms of joy and bliss.

Happiness Affirmations

1. Here and now I cultivate happiness in my life.
2. More and more I am grateful for the blessings in my life, big and small.
3. Each and every day I practice acts of random kindness knowing that giving is it's own reward.
4. I love knowing that I can practice smiling more throughout my day and focus on making a positive difference in the lives of others, and in my life as well.

Feeling Good & Living Great

Happiness Visualization

The Happiness Garden. Begin by assuming a comfortable position. Spend a few moments relaxing any tense areas in your physical body. Do not do a complete relaxation, rather concentrate on problem spots only. When you are finished, gently close your eyes.

Begin by imagining your emotional body as a garden. Get the complete experience of the garden by using all your senses. First, note what the garden looks like. Notice the colors and types of plants. Observe the overall and specific condition of the garden. Is it ordered and well kept, or chaotic and gangly?

Listen for any sounds in your garden made by the wind, or by various animals in the garden. Notice the texture and feel of the various plants in your garden. Are any plants coarse, prickly, soft, velvety, hard, etc.? Become aware of other things in the garden, such as the dirt, the sun, the air, any smells, and so forth.

Now, as the gardener, focus on any areas of your garden which are out of balance or are not bringing you happiness and joy. Look for any weeds or plants that are unhealthy, wild or tangled. Notice how these plants effect the rest of the garden. For example, are the weeds overwhelming and strangling all other areas of your garden? Are unhealthy plants making it difficult for other plants to grow?

As you contemplate the state of your garden, begin to see how the plants symbolize your feelings and thoughts. What negative emotions and thoughts might you be harboring that are like weeds choking the life, beauty, and joy from the other plants? How do any sick and unhealthy plants represent positive potentials in yourself that you have neglected? How could you nourish them more so they bring greater happiness and joy into your life? Or, how are tangled areas symbolic of states of confusion, or karmic situations that you need to resolve, in order for your garden of happiness to grow?

After you have taken some time to assess the state of your garden and have received insights regarding the mental and emotional states they symbolize, set the intent to put your garden in order so more happiness grows there. Begin with the weeds. Slowly pull each weed out of your garden. Make sure to get it by its roots. Notice if some weeds are easier to pull than others. As you pull the weeds try to identify the negative thoughts and emotions associated with them. Then move to the tangled parts of your garden. Set your intent to order and sort these plants out, and as you do so see your thoughts and feelings entering into a greater state of freedom and joy. Continue to move throughout your garden pulling out what isn't needed and straightening and strengthening the rest. Spend as much time as you need to.

Now move on to revitalize the depleted areas of your garden. What positive qualities are being neglected there? How if you brought them back to life could you experience greater freedom, happiness, and joy? Bring in whatever you need to in the way of fertilizer, water,

Feeling Good & Living Great

sunshine, and better soil to help bring out the best in your garden. You may even want to plant new plants that represent new thoughts, feelings, and joyful activities you can attract into your life from this point forward.

Conclude by taking time to see, feel, hear, and experience what it would be like to have a healthy, vibrant, beautiful, and joyous garden. Write down your experiences. Repeat this exercise often keeping a log of your progress of allowing your happiness garden to grow.

Happiness Bach Flowers

- Faking Being Happy: Agrimony
- Feeling Unhappy With Yourself: Crab Apple
- Not Able to Find Joy or Peace: Mustard
- Overly Enthused: Vervain
- Drifting Through Life Unhappy: Wild Rose
- Focusing on the Negative: Willow

Part Three

Emotional Rescue Tools

Feeling Good & Living Great

Even though it would be wonderful if you were always able to manage your feelings and emotions well, sometimes you may not. To help you along these lines this chapter provides you with an "emotional emergency response kit." In this kit are a number of tools to help you recover from unhealthy emotional displays. These tools are general and can be applied to all emotional states. Use them with the additional tools given earlier in the book to help you with specific feelings. When you have all of these tools in place and are ready to pull out and use them as needed, then your mastery of various feeling states will dramatically improve.

Support Tools

Many psychologists and doctors attribute a great deal of emotional disorder to stress. There are a number of ways to cope with stress, but one of the best is to have nourishing and loving people surround you during difficult times. In essence these people make up a support system which you can count on to help you get through life. Sadly, in our rapidly changing society many people find themselves cut off from support systems, inclining people to feel lonely, isolated, depressed, and adrift. If this persists for a long period of time, it can lead to serious difficulties.

Jackie understood this. Raised in an emotionally aloof household, Jackie learned early on that it was unsafe and unwise to express herself. When she did she would be criticized. Because of this she felt abandoned and alone in her pain. She also felt ashamed of her anger and fear. Because she had so little support she felt jealous of those who did. When people attempted to get close to her, Jackie would immediately put up walls. If they were able to break down her defenses and develop a relationship with her, she would respond by becoming possessive and afraid that they might leave her. For this reason, she was always vigilant, looking out for people who might threaten her fragile support system and take the one or two people who did support her away from her in life.

In many ways Jackie represents the classic co-dependent person. When you have few people in your life you can trust and go to for support, it is natural to become overly dependent and attached to the few people you do have around you. Fortunately, as Jackie learned to develop trust with a therapist in counseling she was able to work through her fears of other people harming her or taking something (or someone) away from her. She was also able to develop greater discernment so she could see who was, and wasn't, safe for her. Then she could use her anger in a healthy way to stop people from harming her. The more she was able to do this, the more her support system grew. As it did she prospered spiritually, mentally, emotionally, physically, career wise, and financially.

Having helped many people who felt abused, isolated, and unsupported in life I understand that feeling safe as you find a support system is not always easy. You may set the intention to build a support system, but find that your emotions (fear, anger, sorrow, confusion, and jealousy) may stop you. That is why I often encourage people to take baby steps, and if they need to I even help them in finding support in ways that do not always involve individual people. Rather they involve engaging in a variety of activities including social networks, meet up groups, becoming part of a large organization, or being comforted by animals, nature, and spiritual exercises.

Catharsis Tools

At times, as I have already shared, it is important to find a safe way to defuse layers of emotional tension that can build up into triggers. When effectively done, you release emotional energy in a way that is both harmless and vitalizing. When you lack this skill you emote in a way that is unbalanced, destructive, and creates unforeseen negative repercussions. That is why it is important to know how to go through a healthy catharsis. Catharsis can be a great method to purge and cleanse harmful or hurtful emotional states. Ideally, it is not simply a dumping of your emotions onto someone. It is more like a cleansing, a release, and a healing.

In some psychological circles for a time catharsis became a popular method, as people were encouraged to dump their anger and pain into objects like pillows. They were also taught to feel free to vent on other people. Today, internet blogs, YouTube videos, many movies and television shows reinforce this dumping belief. Increasingly people clamor in reality shows and on talk shows to freely share their deep inner pain and rage, putting it on public display. By catharting in this way, people hope to "get it all out." But, often that is not what occurs.

Unfortunately, though the emotions come out, they are rarely resolved. The proof of this can be seen through the lack of healing or cleansing that takes place after this kind of catharsis. Rather than coming closer towards forgiveness, understanding, and compassion with each other, people walk away with bitterness, increased anger, shame, a feeling of superior self-righteousness, or even deeper wounds. Unhealthy catharsis is one reason civil discourse is disintegrating everywhere. People increasingly feel entitled to dump their emotions on others, without having much understanding or training as to how to do this in a healthy way.

Some years ago, Nobel Peace Prize Buddhist monk, Thich Nhat Hanh, spoke to this problem stating that instead of catharting their anger, people were simply reinforcing and practicing how to be increasingly angry as an emotional response. Having at one time worked with troubled teenagers and gang kids, I wrestled with this problem. In some ways it seemed better to have troubled youth pound on pillows than shoot each other with guns, or carve on themselves with knives. But, at the same time unless they learned even more advanced methods of dealing with their emotions in a healthy way, I could see that they were learning to emote without discovering how to cultivate their witness, gain insight into themselves, and catch their emotions at the sensory or feeling levels before they got out of control.

Still, catharsis can be useful especially if it involves a few important components. The first is right motivation. The second is the proper amount of force upon delivery. The third is right timing. These stages can be summarized in a saying I learned many years ago. Before speaking (or catharting) ask yourself, "Is it true? Is it kind? Is it necessary?" Let's examine these three aspects in more detail beginning with right motivation, or the notion of "is it true?"

Motivation. On one level the statement, "Is it true?" asks you to consider if you are speaking your truth and are accurately seeing and understanding the truth of another. This can only be done if you come from the witness standpoint so that you can see the whole picture. Only then can you stand not only in your shoes, but the shoes of another where you can accurately see or consider that person's point of view, motivations and intentions.

Once you are open to the truth of the situation, the motivation to speak that truth helps determine whether you are going through a healthy or unhealthy catharsis. A healthy catharsis of anger for example, is one which states clearly, "I will no longer allow this to occur to me." An unhealthy catharsis is one which states, "You, S.O.B, I am really going to make you pay for all the suffering you put me through." A healthy catharsis of pain is one which says, "I trust you with my pain. I am seeking compassion, forgiveness, and understanding." An unhealthy catharsis says, "I am worthless. I am nothing. Do whatever you want to punish me." Sadly, in our fame driven culture more and more people are being motivated to undergo unhealthy catharsis at times because they believe in doing so they will get attention and notoriety.

Bob discovered the drawbacks of an unhealthy motivation after he learned to cultivate his witness and observe his anger more effectively. For some time he had felt resentful towards his boss for not giving him a promotion he felt he deserved. In part due to anger and depression Bob began to slack off, not performing on the job the way he used to. His attitude was one of "Who cares? Doing well doesn't make a difference around here anyway!"

Though he felt justified in his actions, he couldn't see that his motivation for doing this was really one of revenge. It was his hope by becoming sub-standard in his performance his boss would suffer and look bad. Instead, the person who looked bad was Bob. He not only looked bad, he felt bad. Rather than feeling excited about his work he became lethargic. Over time his usual discipline and productivity slumped. He felt irritable all the time, which in turn resulted in his eating poorly leading in turn to a case of irritable bowl syndrome. Sick, cranky, disgusted and depressed, I helped Bob see how his motivation to hurt his boss was serving no one, and primarily hurting only himself.

As Bob learned more about proper motivation, he discovered how ideally a healthy motivation and catharsis would help him clear the air, achieve greater insight and understanding, and safeguard him by letting others know firmly what he would or would not stand for. All this fosters hope, understanding and unity. Bob saw that his approach was doing none of these. So, one day he sat down with his boss to get greater insight into why he had been overlooked for the promotion. Bob still didn't like what he heard. But, this time instead of sabotaging himself, he cleaned up his work performance, and took the time to find another job. Since he no longer liked where he worked he eventually found a position where he felt more appreciated. He has been happy ever since.

Force. Related to the saying, "Is it kind?" it is important to remember in any catharsis or expression of emotion, the ideal is to as much as possible to remain harmless. Being harmless doesn't mean becoming passive or doing nothing. As Gandhi and Martin Luther King Jr. realized in their non-violent protest movements, you can be harmless and powerful at the same time. That is because when you are forceful in a powerful way you wake people up to a higher and more inclusive way of being.

When catharting it is important to move increasingly towards non-violent and harmless methods. Yes, given the choice it is better to hit someone during an angry outburst than to kill them. Likewise, it is better to hit a pillow than strike out at another human being. And it is better to kill little creatures in a video game than to machine gun down humans on the street. Still, though these forms of physical catharsis discharge emotional tension, they rarely look at the deeper problems underneath, and almost never allow for understanding and compassion to take place.

In the same light, though emotionally or mentally violent methods of catharsis are a substantial step over physical ones, they are still not the healthiest choice. Yes, it is better to call someone names than throw rocks at them when you feel wronged by them. But again, these types of catharsis rarely give you a feeling of long term relief. And, as in physical violence, they often breed bitterness and resentment in those around you who feel pained and angry at you now in return.

That is why as much as possible train yourself to use harmless methods of catharsis. On a physical level get involved in physical exercise, or participate in a mutually agreed upon physical activity to help you discharge the emotional tension (jogging, dancing, tennis, baseball, and so forth). On an emotional level try talking it over with an empathetic person, having a healing cry, or asserting your needs in a clean honest way. On a mental level consider using mindfulness meditation to gain insight. You can even go directly to a spiritual level where understanding and compassion will be a natural response to any emotional crisis you may be in.

Timing. Even though your motivation may be good and you maintain an intention to be harmless, if your timing is off an emotional catharsis can still backfire and cause unwanted damage. Here is where the question, "Is it necessary?" is helpful. Start by asking yourself, "Is it really necessary for me to emotionally cathart here and now?" Also consider, "Is the timing right? Am I in a safe environment with people who will be receptive to my emotional display in the right way? Can they handle it with compassion, understanding, and a lack of judgment? Are the risks for misunderstanding, humiliation, or toxic shaming minimal? Are others in the right space mentally, emotionally, and physically to receive what I have to say in a positive way?"

If not, then reconsider. It may not only be unnecessary to cathart right now, it may actually be unsafe. Remember the end goal is to bring about empathy, compassion and understanding. When people are not prepared or ready for your emotional display or emotional content it comes across as "too much information." For example, to share you were beaten by a spouse with people who know nothing about you, may backfire on you. Instead of feeling empathy for you they may respond with confusion, curiosity, or disgust. They may also ask you inappropriate questions or ridicule you out of their own anxiety and fear of being around someone they perceive as too vulnerable.

As a safe habit then it is best to assume that all people need some sort of warning that you intend to have an emotional catharsis. The best way to do this is to make an initial contact by way of phone or in person to let them know you have something you wish to share, briefly telling them what it may be about. Notice how they respond to your request. If they are reacting or shutting down they are telling you they are not prepared to handle it. Or, they may be able to handle it, but now is not the time or place. If so, ask them when they could be in a compassionate and receptive space. Until they are ready move on to using other tools in your emotional emergency response kit. In doing so, you may even discover that the need to cathart no longer exists.

Centering Tools

When you have matured in your emotional expression the predominating qualities within your feeling state will be those of patience, calm, poise, satisfaction, and measured and healthy emotional response. This ability to be poised and calm when working with your feelings can only be achieved as you carry within your overall emotional field a posture of assurance, confidence, and self esteem. It is therefore vitally important to work on solidifying your emotional field and one of the best ways of doing this is through centering.

Of the many centering tools available one of the best involves conscious breathing. When working on a suicide hotline many years ago I was often struck by how breathy and short individual's breathing rhythms were while speaking about their suicidal ideations. By simply recommending that they take deep diaphragmatic steady breaths while talking to me, I was able time and again to substantially stabilize their depressed mood and move them increasingly into a state of calm.

Breathing from the Diaphragm. Here are some tips

Feeling Good & Living Great

to see if you are breathing from the diaphragm:

1. Place your hands just below your ribcage on each side of your body, fingers forward, thumbs back. As you inhale notice whether or not your hands are being pushed outward. If yes, you are breathing from your diaphragm. If no, you are breathing from a different place.
2. Lie down and place a book on your stomach region just below your rib cage. Breathe naturally. Notice if the book is pushed up or not. If yes, you are breathing from your diaphragm. If no, place the book either on your chest, or below your navel. See if you are breathing from one of these places instead.

<u>Centering Breathing Exercise</u>. Once you know where your diaphragm is and how to breathe from there consider practicing the following basic breathing exercise as a means of centering yourself.

1. Sit in a comfortable chair with your spine erect and with your feet flat on the floor.
2. Bring your attention to your diaphragm and slowly begin to breathe from this space gently and naturally.
3. As you continue to breathe relax your shoulders, jaw, and eye muscles. If need be, breathe in through your nose and out through your mouth. (Note: you tend to breathe out through your mouth when you have heavy emotional issues you are attempting to process.

Sighing is often a reflection of this).
4. As you continue to breathe, just be aware of the rising and falling of your breath. Notice how high your breath rises on the inbreath. Does it stop at your lower chest, upper chest, or throat? As you let your breath go notice if your exhale is long and slow, quick, heavy, or strained? Also see if you can be sensitive to how the air goes in and out through your nose and/or mouth. Just watch your breath without judgment.
5. Now, as you breathe in attempt to gently open up or expand the area where you feel your breath stops. Do not force the process. Let your body respond as it needs to. Whereever you feel blocked mentally confirm to yourself, "I'm ok. I am loved." Or, say to yourself softly, "Be myself, renew."
6. On the exhale, see if you can spend more time exhaling in a slow and steady way. As you do embrace yourself and say silently, "Let go, relax." Or, if it is more soothing say, "I'm all right. I can handle this."
7. Repeat this final inhale and exhale process for approximately two to three minutes until you feel more peaceful and calm. At no time attempt to force the process in a way that makes you feel uncomfortable.
8. Close the exercise by breathing naturally again without conscious thought as to where or how you are breathing. Simply rest in the sensation of peace.

The advantage of doing this practice often is that

you will not only feel more calm and relaxed, you will also feel more revitalized and energized. The end result? You will not only feel good, you will be in a better position to live great as you are able to approach the ups and downs of life in a steady, positive, and proactive way.

Law of Attraction Tools

As a law of attraction teacher and author of a bestselling book on the topic (*Beyond the Secret: Spiritual Power and the Law of Attraction*), I understand a lot about how what you see, or believe, sets up a whole chain of responses based upon how you condition yourself in these ways. Affirmations and visualization exercises are helpful as a means of consciously reconditioning your brain and nervous systems to respond in new and more appropriate ways. That is why in the previous chapters I included affirmations and a visualization exercises to use with each of the major emotional states. But, for now, I want you to simply get a basic understanding of how learning to consciously program yourself for success in handling these feelings through affirmations and visualizations can be an important tool for you.

So why do so many people carry negative conditioning and beliefs? Most likely because they have undergone a series of traumatic events, particularly in their early formative years. That is why changing people's beliefs and behaviors is rarely as easy as telling them to do so. Why? Because traumatic events threaten their safety, security, and survival. If the trauma is sudden and they don't know how to cope, traumatized people end up feeling powerless. Often their minds shut down or go adrift in a state of confusion. And, their emotions become flat, depressed, or hyper-sensitive (because their nervous system keeps them in a state of being hyper-alert).

That is why getting to someone who has been traumatized right away so they can receive empathy for their suffering, and regain a sense of trust, perspective, and direction is crucial. When this healing does not take place traumatic episodes entrench maladaptive thoughts, feelings, and behaviors into the brains of trauma victims often cultivating in them a helpless and fearful stance towards life. Instead of healing, they relive the trauma over and over again. Like digging open a scab once a wound is almost healed, they inadvertently keep inflicting pain on themselves when they do this. Instead, of healing, scar tissue is created, damaging them far beyond the pain incurred by the original traumatic events.

Traumatic episodes can also cause a cascade effect of self-doubt, self-blame, shame, and self-abuse which have nothing to do with the traumatic event. For example, Elsie who was raped by a stranger at a very young age began to attack and doubt her right to be attractive, or to have a healthy relationship with someone. Sadly, she even blamed herself for the rape asking herself through a misguided use of law of attraction techniques how she could have attracted such an awful event into her life. The truth was she was just unconscious and naïve. She trusted in a man to care for her who ended up harming her instead. (Note: I have confronted and often countered this "victim is always to blame" teaching associated with the law of attraction in my best-selling book *Beyond the Secret: Spiritual Power and the Law of Attraction*).

Tony went through a different traumatic event when he was fired from a job. With his confidence shaken he began to doubt his skills, blame himself for having chosen a particular field of employment, and hid his need for support from his loved ones since he was ashamed of appearing weak. Because of this he went into a state of emotional numbness and chronic unemployment that ended as he took on a series of dead-end jobs that were far beneath his true skills.

In both examples, even though these traumas happened years ago, both people still lived within a traumatized state that was reinforced by the cultivation of destructive thoughts, feelings, and behaviors. Through therapy these were reprogrammed as the story they told themselves about these events was transformed. Feelings of violation and rejection were also eventually replaced with hope and validation. For Elsie that meant believing and feeling that she could once again be attractive, feel safe, trust men, and take healthy and safe risks when meeting prospective partners. For Tony it meant discovering that his talents could in fact be utilized, he could finally be rewarded for being creative, and he could take calculated chances in advancing his career or improving his work environment.

In addition, the wisdom from each trauma was gleaned along with a state of being more forgiving and compassionate towards themselves and others. In time, both learned how these very same traumas gave them greater wisdom and empathy in relation to the overall human condition. In dong so both found it deepened their spiritual approach in life. And, finally, affirmations and visualizations were used to help them reshape the direction of their lives, helping them to feel good and live great in their lives once more.

Spiritual Tools

At last we come to the final, and yet the most important tools for helping you achieve mastery over your feeling states — the spiritual tools. They are considered spiritual because they consciously help you develop the qualities of love, light, spiritual power and divine understanding. Of the many spiritual tools you can use, the ones I find most helpful are meditation and prayer.

As for meditation techniques they are numerous. (Look for my book *Meditation: The Path to Peace* to learn more). Two are especially helpful for mastering feeling states. One is the technique of mindfulness. Here you utilize the witness to calmly observe your thoughts and feelings in a state of non-judgment. Instead of attempting to figure why you are having an emotional reaction, you simply witness and embrace it. There is great healing potential in this approach as you learn to observe whatever feeling state arises (hopelessness, despair, anger, pain), in a compassionate way.

The other type of meditation practice that I find most helpful is insight meditation. Unlike in a mindfulness meditation, here you do attempt to root out and make visible the underlying causes of your emotional patterns. An example of this kind of meditation practice follows:

1. Sit in a comfortable chair with your spine erect and your feet on the floor. You can also sit with your legs supporting you in a cross-legged position. Then, gently close your eyes.
2. Allow your attention to come to your breathing, simply watching the natural rhythm of your breath rise and fall.
3. Next, allow your physical body to gradually relax. Make sure you are not hunching your shoulders. Let your stomach hang out as it needs to without letting a belt or tension constrict it. As you scan for areas of tension and seek to relax them pay particular attention to keeping the jaw relaxed, the forehead and cheek muscles, as well as the tiny muscles around the eyes.
4. Now, visualize your emotions as a calm pool of clear water. As you continue to breathe naturally, allow any ripples of emotional upset to smooth out. Let yourself be in a place of emotional peace for the moment.
5. When you feel emotionally calm, take three steady, deep, and diaphragmatic breaths. With each breath lift your focus of attention upwards to the place

approximately three inches in front of the physical forehead. Using your creative imagination see a small golden sun forming there.
6. As the light of this sun intensifies, imagine this light being thrown downward and outward so that it slowly envelopes your entire physical body and extends some inches beyond it. Let this light slowly seep into every pore of your body, gently illumining your brain and nervous system. Remember at this point to keep this a sensorial experience and not a thinking one.
7. After completing this process, direct this light to illuminate a particular area in your life that you are having difficulty with. Slowly allow your thought processes to be activated. Gently let an insight or two come into your awareness. Do not force the process.
8. Continue to stay with the flow of insights for approximately five to ten minutes. If no insights arise, stay within the sensation of light and know they will come of their own accord later. Upon completion of this exercise, gently open your eyes and write down any insights which may have occurred. Take your time as you come out of the meditation, as some people may feel a little disoriented after doing so.

Finally, before I close this section I would like to offer a few prayers that I find particularly useful when it comes to handling emotions well. Both are prayers that help bring about emotional stability and peace. The first is from the Native American tradition. Though the word beauty is used within it, you can replace that word with others such as love, peace, joy, wisdom, contentment and so forth. The second prayer is a standard one frequently used in the Alcoholics Anonymous tradition.

A Native American Prayer.

With beauty before me, I walk.
With beauty behind me, I walk.
With beauty above me, I walk.
With beauty below me, I walk.
From the East, beauty has been restored.
From the South, beauty has been restored.
From the West, beauty has been restored.
From the North, beauty has been restored.
From the zenith in the sky beauty has been restored.
From the nadir of the earth beauty has been restored.
From all around me beauty has been restored.

Serenity Prayer.

God grant me the serenity to accept the things I cannot change, courage to change the things I can, and the wisdom to know the difference — *Author Unknown.*

Summary

After putting together your "emotional emergency response kit," you can also serve yourself by agreeing to the following premises. One, commit to the belief that no matter what emotional reactions you display, you are in essence good, and therefore worthy of compassion, love, and kindness as a human being. Two, anytime you succumb to an unhealthy emotional display agree to move beyond guilt into forgiveness. The ability to forgive does not negate responsibility for your actions, it simply empowers you to overcome guilt by making a commitment to become a better human being.

Three, learn to listen to what is really going on with you on an emotional level. Practice registering emotions as much as possible at the sensorial or feeling level. Fourth, commit to using the many tools available in this book to help you think, question, and discern what is going on with you at an emotional level. Fifth, agree to make mastery of your feeling states an important priority in your everyday life. Only in this way can mastery become a reality and not simply another well intentioned, but theoretical experience.

Putting It All Together

Feeling Good & Living Great

Congratulations! Throughout this book you have been given a variety of ideas and techniques to help you feel good and live great by learning how to master various feeling states. Now, it is time to put those techniques together so that you can access them at any time to help you manage your feeling states in such a way you can keep them at the healthy levels. And, by keeping them in as healthy a state as you are able to, you will feel good and live great for the larger majority of your life.

The Complete Master Plan

1. As much as possible learn to handle your feeling states as the witness, or observer.
2. Regularly learn to disidentify so that you understand who you really are as the witness, and how you have thoughts, feelings, or actions, but you are not your thoughts, feelings, or actions.
3. Become a mentally polarized individual. This is best done by remembering that your true identity is one of a spiritual being. As that spiritual being spend time cultivating the four levels of mind learning to utilize each in a healthy way.
4. Anchored in the above begin to handle your feeling states at the level of sensation before they become feelings and emotions.
5. If you are unable to do they will shift to the level of feeling. There do your best to work with them at the healthy level or at least within the average range.

6. At the level of feeling take time to identify what the main feeling is. If need be start out with whether it is hot or cold. Then attempt to identify the specific feeling state in terms of one of the six major emotions.
7. After you identify which major feeling state you are working with, see if you are coming from the healthy, average, or unhealthy levels in regards to that feeling.
8. Review the gift, costs, and questions that feeling is attempting to reveal to you.
9. Choose one or more of the techniques provided to help you raise that feeling state to a healthy level so you can cultivate its gift.
10. Practice the affirmations, visualizations, and use the Bach flower remedies as needed to help you lift the feeling to the healthy level and to allow you to re-engage the higher levels of your mind, as well as to step back into being the observer or witness.
11. If you are unable to master your feelings at the healthy level and they slip into emotional reactions then do your best to diffuse your own emotional reactions by following the steps outlined on page 72.
12. Also, make a commitment to become better at going through the master plan so that you will be less likely to sink into emotionally reactive states.

Summary of the Feeling States for Easy Reference

Fear Gift and Questions to Contemplate.
- Fear is overcome through knowledge and deepening

your capacity to love.
- In what areas do I need to increase my knowledge so I can cope with and eliminate my fear effectively?
- How can I learn to love what I fear so I can move it into a positive direction?

Fear Techniques.
- Deep Breathing.
- Desensitization.
- Reduce Stimulation.
- Unify With Your Fear.
- Cultivate Courage.

Confusion Gift and Questions to Contemplate.
- Confusion brings clarity regarding your true calling and direction.
- How do I need to surrender and let Spirit guide me through this process?
- How can I relax and live more in the moment so I can better open up to what Spirit is wanting from me?

Confusion Techniques.
- Rest.
- Learn from the Past.
- Live in the Now.
- Risk.
- Consciously Complain.

Sorrow Gift and Questions for Contemplation.

- Sorrow opens you up to greater insight, humility and compassion.
- What do I need to let go of at this point in my life before I attract something new?
- What lessons do I need to learn that will help me use this loss in a soulful way?

Sorrow Techniques.
- Cry.
- Exercise.
- Talk.
- Book and Movie Therapy.
- Avoid Depression.

Anger Gift and Questions for Contemplation.
- Anger implores you to set boundaries and establish respect.
- Where do I feel misunderstood, disrespected, and in danger at this moment?
- What do I need to communicate to someone to help me feel understood, respected, safe and secure?

Anger Techniques.
- Meditate.
- Set Boundaries.
- Forgive.
- Take Responsibility.
- Don't Tolerate Abuse.

Feeling Good & Living Great

Jealousy Gift and Questions for Contemplation.
- Jealousy helps you get clear about what you most desire in life.
- Where do I lack faith and insight to help me get what I really want?
- What do I need to let go of so I can better attract what Spirit really wants for me?

Jealousy Techniques.
- Don't Feed Irrational Beliefs.
- Manage Your Projections.
- Have Faith.
- Learn to Appreciate.
- Get Clear About Your Wants and Don't Wants.

Happiness Gift and Questions for Contemplation.
- Happiness lightens you up and fuels you with energy so you can move forward.
- How can I get back in touch with what gives me pleasure and cultivate more of it in my life?
- How can I laugh, smile, and feel more at choice regarding how I live in this present moment?

Happiness Techniques.
- Smile.
- Cultivate Gratitude.
- Laugh.
- Feel Good Tool Kit.
- Love.

ABOUT DR. LISA LOVE

Dr. Lisa Love is the best-selling author of *Beyond the Secret* and a counselor with five degrees in Marriage, Family, and Child Counseling, as well as Spiritual Psychology and Transpersonal Psychology. Using her extensive training and experience she helps others through individual and group coaching programs as well as writes, speaks and gives workshops on joy, spirituality, love, relationships, dating and the spiritual use of the law of attraction. She also helps people REACH to become *Rapidly Evolving Agents for Changing Humanity*.™ She does this by helping them make dramatic breakthroughs so they can live more soulful and truly meaningful lives. Mostly she helps her clients cultivate empathy and compassion for all of their life experience so they can live in a state of joy, peace of mind, health and love.

- Founder
    - *REACH programs*
    - *LoveMovies!*
    - *Soul to Spirit*
- Author
    - *Beyond the Secret*
    - *Feeling Good & Living Great*
    - *How NOT to Love Yourself*
    - *Meditation: The Path to Peace*
    - *Attracting Real Love*
- Former
    - *Match.com* dating advisor
    - *America Online* teacher
- **Websites & Social Media**:
    - www.doctorlisalove.com
    - www.facebook.com/drlisalove
    - www.twitter.com/doctorlisalove
    - www.youtube.com/doctorlisalove
- Media and radio personality
- *LiveAdvice.com* top counselor
- Syndicated columnist
- Counselor and coach with over 25 years experience
- Owner of 5 psychology & counseling degrees

Beyond the Secret
Spiritual Power
& the Law of Attraction

By Dr. Lisa Love

The greatest secret isn't know how to wish; it's knowing what to wish for!

"Reading this book will help you find happiness and when you do, you will be a success." — Bernie Siegel, MD

Yes, you can have anything you want. Especially when you are coming from Spirit as you do the wishing. A best-selling book with over 30,000 copies in print and now in 5 languages, **BEYOND THE SECRET**, explains how to use the law of attraction in a spiritually powerful way. Says Dr. Love, "The law of attraction is more than the power of positive thinking or a think and grow rich plan. When the abundance (be it love, health, wealth or whatever) is approved by Spirit, then it will also be guided by Spirit. And this is the key to *keeping* what we want, not just attracting it. That is what happens when the abundance you attract serves more than our own individual good; and contributes to the good of others, as well as for the well being of the entire world."

- **Best-selling book** now in its **3rd Printing**!
- Learn the **Ten Step Process** that helps you attract what Spirit most wants for you to have in life.
- Discover how to attract and transform **"you" into "YOU"** or your higher spiritual self so your wishes and desires are anchored in spiritual principles.
- Get access to **over 30 practical techniques** that help you manifest what you want in life in a spiritual way.
- Discover your **spiritual purpose** for being here.
- Start NOW to attract more of what Spirit really wants for to **live a truly loving and fulfilling life!**

To Order Book Please Visit: www.doctorlisalove.com

Feeling Good & Living Great
How Handling Any Feeling Well Helps You Live a Better Life

By Dr. Lisa Love

Learn how to feel good and live great by realizing how every feeling has gift to give you if used in a spiritual way. In short, anger, sorrow, jealousy, confusion, fear, and happiness are all there for a reason. When used in a positive way they show you how to live great, no matter what the circumstances in your life!

Here is just some of what you will learn in this book…

1. How to turn your:
    - **Anger into Energy** — to make the changes you need to.
    - **Sorrow into Compassion** — by increasing your empathy for self and others.
    - **Fear into Love** — by gaining knowledge and wisdom to handle life well.
    - **Confusion into Clarity** — giving you a positive direction in life.
    - **Jealousy into Fulfillment** — through confidence that you can have what you want.
    - **Happiness into Joy** — where you feel good by doing good for yourself and others.
2. How to create an **"Emotional Rescue Kit"** that you can pull out and use quickly when you lose it emotionally bringing yourself back into balance and harmony.
3. How to **attract more of what you want** because your emotions no longer get in the way.

In short I know the **200 pgs of rich material** in this book will help you. Consider buying it now!

To Order Book Please Visit: www.doctorlisalove.com

Attracting Real Love
5 Simple Steps for Getting the Love You Want

By Dr. Lisa Love

You Are About to Experience All the Love You Really Want to Feel....

No more heartbreak, loneliness, uncertainty, or disappointment -- just love, *real* love from now on. How? By changing your focus from finding someone out there to love you to putting the focus on thoroughly loving yourself. And, by learning what love really is so you can attract it to yourself.

It's true, most people don't have love in their lives, because they confuse love for lust, infatuation, addiction, neediness, codependency, and even abuse. But, it doesn't have to be that way when you know love really is and how to attract it to.

Here is just some of what you will learn in this book...

- It will reveal to you **how to become a real "lover" of yourself and others**.
- It will clearly help you **understand "false" versus "real" love** on love on all levels: spiritual, personal, mental, emotional, physical, and sexual.
- It will show you **how love is deeply connected to attachment and intimacy**. In fact, the lack of both of these in your life in an empowering and healthy way is typically the major root cause behind all disappointing experiences in the realm of love.
- As you continue to understand what real love is, you will also **get a new awareness of the role of romance as viewed by men, and also by women.**
- And, if your present relationship is in trouble, or you have just lost one, this book gives **practical advise on how to radically improve your relationship.**

To Order Book Please Visit: www.doctorlisalove.com

How NOT to Love Yourself
Misguided Teachings From the Princess Realms

By Dr. Lisa Love

Discover the mistakes nine fairy tale princesses make in their desperate quest for love. Then learn how not to make these mistakes yourself to create a true chance for a happy ever after full of *real* love, by learning how to really love yourself.

Here is just some of what you will learn in this book…

- Change your focus from putting others first to **putting yourself first** so by loving yourself so you can love others.
- Stop sleep walking through life waiting for your "prince" to come and learn **how to get conscious so you can lead a happy full life** instead.
- Stop playing dumb or naïve out of fear of facing the world, and **develop the maturity and wisdom you need to protect yourself** and surround yourself with loving people.
- Remove the tendency to give away your many talents and change yourself unfairly in an attempt to attract a partner so that you **respect your true talents and gifts** and attract someone who love you for you!
- No longer tolerate beastly behaviors in men by making excuses for them, and **learn to teach others to treat you well** loving yourself enough to attract real love to you.
- Discover ways you may be unwittingly giving your power away to others, and **learn to retain your personal power** so that you can live the life you are meant to.
- Find other ways to cope with life besides checking out in destructive ways so that you can **courageously face reality and live a life that is truly meaningful and free.**
- And, much, much, more!

To Order Book Please Visit: www.doctorlisalove.com

Meditation
The Path to Peace

By Dr. Lisa Love

This book is a summary of my years of practicing and teaching meditation to students locally as a teacherof meditation online through *America Online's* Online Campus.

Early in my life I discovered the many enormous benefits of meditation. And, I discovered it was a way to reveal your true spiritual identity, calm and focus your mind, and master your emotions so they are tranquil and peaceful. That is why I have practiced and even taught various forms of meditation practices for decades. At one point I even meditated four hours straight a day for a period of two years. This extensive spiritual practice even led me an in-depth understanding of just how far meditation practice can take you in discovery your true self.

- Get a clear understanding of **What Meditation Is** in both the classical and modern definition of it.
- Learn the **Eight Benefits of Meditation** that come about when you use various meditation techniques and how they can help you at all levels (spiritually, personally, mentally, emotionally, vitally, physically).
- Discover various **Types of Meditation Practice** so you can choose the meditation that is best for you.
- Find out how various practice can aid the **Various Levels of Your Being** (spiritually, personally, mentally, emotionally, vitally, physically).
- Know what is required in the way of **Meditation Aids** including setting up the right location and conditions for your meditation practice.
- **Get Started for Meditation Practice** in an effortless way so it becomes beneficial and easy for you.
- Get training in **Meditation Exercises** that can give you the best foundation for beginning, intermediate, and advanced meditation practices.

To Order Book Please Visit: www.doctorlisalove.com

REACH Programs

By Dr. Lisa Love

- Are you ready to be free?
- Are you are ready to change your life?
- Are you ready to embrace yourself and others with love and compassion?
- Are you ready to rid yourself of limitations preventing you from being who you *really* are and accomplishing what you are here for?
- Are you ready to **REACH** - to become a *Rapidly Evolving Agent for Changing Humanity™?*

If so, join others who are dedicating themselves to a new way of living based on increased conscious awareness of self and others resulting in a culture of compassion, unity, empathy, harmony, and love. Discover how powerful you can be, and how much more joyful you will feel when you integrate all aspects of who you are.

Seven Main REACH Programs

- Conscious Security - Trusting Life to Provide for You
- Conscious Pleasure: Enjoying Life in Healthy Ways
- Conscious Power—Living With Vigor to Fulfill Your Life Purpose
- Conscious Loving: Using Real Love to Cultivate Loving Relationships
- Conscious Communication: Standing in Integrity & Truth
- Conscious Vision: Creating a Life of Peace & Love
- Conscious Unity: Experiencing Oneness as the Essence of Love

Trainings happen individually, in group format, online, and in person. Join us!

To Learn More Please Visit: www.doctorlisalove.com

www.ingramcontent.com/pod-product-compliance
Lightning Source LLC
Chambersburg PA
CBHW071706090426
42738CB00009B/1679